Annette Edwards

Jan 21, 2004

A SAGA OF A CHEECHAKO CLAN

AN AUTOBIOGRAPHY BY

ANNETTE ALDERSON EDWARDS

Library of Congress Card Number: 2001118780

ISBN 0-9713085-0-0

Printed in the USA by
Morris Publishing
3212 East Highway 30 •
Kearney, NE 68847 • 800-650-7888

ACKNOWLEDGEMENTS

To my mother, who wanted me to write about our travels long before her death. She would have enjoyed reading this. This is a family history that my grandchildren will enjoy reading to their children one day.

I want to thank Julie Mahan for getting me started on writing my autobiography and my daughter, Denise, for her help with this. Thanks to my son, Garry, for putting the finishing touches in the right places. And, of course, my three friends, Alene Ott, Della Purdue and Bettie Marshall, that have heard my stories so many times before.

CONTENTS

Chapter 1

Early Memories

As I sit here surrounded by aged oak trees, and dazzling red azaleas gracing the north side of my home, my mind keeps wandering back to the ragged hills of Arkansas. Could it be because I'm aging and wonder what my life could have been if I had made my permanent home in Alaska? My husband, Jim, is now a retired pilot, with years of experience as a bush pilot in Alaska. After returning to the U. S. he flew executive flying for a number of years before his heart attack which grounded him from flying. He never knew he had the skills of a carpenter that would be useful in later life. He checked out a book from the library that would guide him through the basic building of a house. He knew he could construct a house just as strong and sturdy as he could an airplane. Since Jim is retired now, he can put all of his energy in building our retirement home. As we drove around the countryside each day we would keep a sharp eye out for suitable acreage for our purpose. We located two acres that was full of pine and oak trees on this straight and noiseless road that was well suited for our home.

We had fun planning the layout for our modified A-frame. We finally came up with a floor plan that we both agreed on. We started preparing the foundation. Each week we could see progress. With the added dormer, it ended up having twenty-two hundred square feet including the upstairs. You can see how much room I have on the second floor. It includes an elevator that takes me up to my favorite hide-a-way. He wrapped a deck around the front and one side of the downstairs and a deck upstairs for my escape route in case of fire.

Jim built a large workshop south of our dwelling where he could rebuild airplanes. Houses here are far enough apart that if I chose to holler at Jim I could without the neighbors knowing what I yelled about. I'd say I had it made. Well, almost. My son, Garry, and my son-in-law, Dan purchased a computer to grace my new office on the second floor. I have an oversize bathroom and guest room on the north end and a large bedroom that opens out into my office on the south side.

One day Jim told me not to come to the shop because he was working on something that I had been nagging him about. Temptation took over and of course I looked.

One lazy afternoon when I arrived home from a luncheon with my friends I was thrilled to see Jim setting up a swing under my favorite gnarled oak. He walked off smiling and soon returned with two glasses of iced tea. He always stood so straight and had thick brown wavy hair that I used to run my fingers through in our courting days. As he came closer his shoulders were slightly bent. His hair had turned silvery white years ago. His bent shoulders are probably caused by his many years of tinkering in his shop and his recent triple bypass. I can see in his eyes that his health is failing him. Those baby blue eyes would just melt me away when we were dating. They are not as strong as they once were. They seem to be fading as the months swiftly fly by. The years have taken their toll on both of us. I'm glad we're able to take care of each other.

If I had routed my life differently, would it have been better? One can only guess. I certainly have been tempted to wander off in many directions, but the love of my family kept me in close range. I have seen much, done a lot and some I wish I could do over, but that's life. You can't turn around and redo the mistakes you've made in the past, but I made a solemn promise that I'd try to improve.

As Jim handed me the tea he said, "Little Missy (my nick-name) you have always wanted to write, so I thought you would like to sit here and let the birds charm you while your thoughts wander back to yesteryear as you pen your favorite tales."

"Do you have anything in mind that you would like to write about?" he asked as the breeze blew gently through his thinning hair.

"Yes I do. It will be interesting to see what I can drag up from my earliest memories," I said. A squirrel was playing overhead. It seemed as if he was purposely knocking acorns down on us. Jim went in to refill my glass before he went back to his shop. How refreshing. He knew I enjoyed thinking back on the years I spent in Alaska. The last six years were with him and our children. I wouldn't take anything for the years I spent there.

When he returned I said, "Jim, do you wish we had stayed in that great frontier land? You taught me not to be afraid of flying when I was with you. We went to many fly-in breakfasts in different areas that were near Anchorage. Remember when we flew on the other side of the inlet and landed on a dry riverbed? You wanted to check out this old abandoned cabin. It was interesting. It still had some cups and plates scattered around the place, and too, a bear might have paid a visit and tore the place up."

As he got up to leave me with my thoughts he looked back at me with that cute sideways grin he has.

"I have more rib stitching to do on the last plane wing. When you run out of tea let me know," he said as he ambled into the shop.

It's great that he can continue working with something he loves to do. I went to my office to get my erasable ink pen and plenty of paper and a pillow for my back and return to the swing. I leaned back on my pillow and made myself comfortable. I sat there for awhile deep in thought. Swinging so gently can have a hypnotizing effect on you. I started thinking about so much of my past life. My brothers and I can look back on our lives in the country and still have a lot of laughs.

My mother had told me how large she had gotten with her pregnancy, carrying at least two babies. How Frankie and I had broken one of her ribs while we were wrestling in her body, just before our birth. I suppose I was trying to beat Frankie out into this unknown world we would be entering shortly.

Doctor McCown and his nurse made their journey on this cold, dreary morning to deliver Frankie and me. Dr. McCown went to Mom's room to make preparations for this event and was surprised to see that all was in order. Dad and a friend were waiting at Mom's bedside as he came closer to say "Hi Miss Katie" and to check the actual signs for the delivery. When Mom let out her first scream Dad ran out to another part of the house. He knew he would pass out if he stayed there. Come to think of it, I probably took my fainting spells from him. Dad heard a slap on a bottom and a little cry. He was pacing the floor when the Doctor came out of Mom's room and told him he had a baby girl. This bespectacled little man pulled his pipe from his pocket and filled it with tobacco. He struck a match and lit the pipe when he heard Mom scream. The nurse threw open the door and told the Doctor, "You better come quick, there's another one on the way." The Doctor crammed the pipe in his pocket as he ran back to deliver the second baby. Do you think that was me kicking and squirming around because Frankie beat me out! Mom told me which one of us was first but I long forgot what she said. Dad was already jittery when the Doctor came out and told him he had another girl. Doctor McCown went back to Mom's bedside and held her hand and she looked up at him with a smile and he said, "Katie, you have two beautiful baby girls."

When the Doctor showed up at the door the third time smiling he noticed smoke coming from his pocket. He had forgotten that he put the lit pipe in his pocket when he went in to deliver the second baby. After getting the smoke under control, Dad just looked at him and said, "The hell you say, not another one!" I wonder if Dad could have handled triplets.

Early Memories

Frankie Bell and Annette Elizabeth came into this world January 4, 1923 kicking and screaming. We weighed just a little over three pounds each. Our first diapers were my Dad's handkerchiefs. Our beds were two large shoeboxes with soft warm covers in them. Remember back in those days, January was a pretty cold month. Mom kept us warm by the wood stove. If she hadn't taken special care of us we probably wouldn't have made it through the winter.

Mom and Dad had their first girl September 24, 1920, two years and four months before we showed up on the scene and named her Beulah Pearl. Now Dad had three girls. He was thrilled over the new twins. Mom wasn't thinking about much of anything at the time. She was completely exhausted and I can see why.

Dad had fun with us. I can recall an event when we were about three. He took Frankie, Pearl and me to the circus one Saturday. We sat on the front row and a clown with colorful baggy pants and a painted face with a large red nose came by tossing balls into the air. We thought he was hilarious until one hit the top of his head and water shot straight up. Frankie and I thought it came out of the clown's head. We were so scared we jumped in Dad's lap. He hugged us close and told us that he was just a clown and was suppose to do silly things to make kids laugh. Pearl thought everything was funny. She wouldn't let anything like a clown bother her, not even at the age of five.

I can recall the day Dad took Frankie and me to the cotton gin one Saturday to show off his little girls. His friend that worked there also had twin girls the same age as we were. Frankie and I were identical but they weren't. Their names were Dorothy and Doris Nolan. Dorothy had olive skin and dark hair and Doris had fair skin and blonde hair. After entering school, they were our good friends for many years. Doris died later at age sixteen. I saw Dorothy for the last time in Forrest City about ten years ago. She and one of her sisters were retiring in a town north of Miami, Florida. Now both of them are gone.

Mom started training us girls in our table manners long before school age. Later when my brothers were old enough they would pull our chairs out for us girls and push them back as we sat down. We would help Mom set the table. Oh, we knew it all at an early age. Whatever happened to that young training? At my age now one may wonder, "who cares." I recall getting the broom out to sweep the kitchen or dining room floor. Mom would brag on my achievements. She knew I needed this attention to keep me motivated. Somehow I would balk a lot. I suppose that came along with my shyness. We loved Mom. I can still see her with Pearl in her lap and Frankie and me on her well used rocking chair arms and her going back and forth ever so gentle and singing to us in that sweet soft voice. She could carry a good tune. I can think back on one song that I loved to hear her sing by the name of "When You and I Were Young, Maggie." It kinda makes your eyes want to go misty, doesn't it?

The first house that comes to my mind was in Palestine, Arkansas in 1927. Dad was the sawyer for Mr.Young, the owner of the sawmill. Mr.Young had quite a large mill operation. Dad was the best in his field. When a truckload of lumber was delivered to a Memphis lumberyard they never had to ask where it came from. They knew Dad's lumber; it always had a perfect cut. That truly was his talent. That man was one of the best with trees and lumber. He could walk through the woods and tell you exactly how many feet he could get out of the whole lot.

There was a flood the summer we lived in Palestine. The 1927 flood got up to our porch, but didn't get in the house. Dad bought a boat and tied it to the porch post for us to evacuate, in case the water rose higher. I've seen Mom stand on the front porch and shoot the heads off of snakes as they swam near our house. She could shoot a snake between the eyes, twenty yards away, as one would swim closer to our house. Woe to anything that got in the sight of Mom and her faithful rifle. I wish many times that she had kept it. I have often wondered what happened to her rifle. She kept most everything else that would fit in her trunks that was hauled around with us. Mom got rid of many things that she wouldn't need again when we left those hills and the rifle was one of them.

Dad's boss, Mr. Young, had a twelve year old boy, Standish, that made a log wagon and told us girls we could play with it anytime we wanted to. The wagon was rough looking but we still thought that it was the prettiest wagon on four wheels. The boy wasn't bad looking either. Right after the flood had receded and the ground started drying out, we girls started playing outside again. Pearl asked Mom if we could go see Standish. She said we could but warned us about the narrow bridge that we had to cross to get to his house. When we entered the yard, Standish was checking his wagon. It was a rugged looking thing with four wheels, but he was proud of it. He told us we could take the wagon to our house and play with it as long as we wanted to. So we headed home with wagon in tow.

He made his wagon out of rough lumber that he had picked up at his Dad's mill. He located a small log that he wrestled with one day, sawing four rounds off for his wheels. He punched holes in the center of each round. Put an iron rod through the holes and attached them in the proper place on the wagon. He was really proud of his newly found talents in the construction line. But it was hard to pull or push. We thought maybe Uncle Jessie, who was visiting us at the time, could put some grease or oil on each wheel so we could manage the thing better. We had to go back across this bridge where the floodwater was still pretty high.

We got halfway across the bridge and Pearl decided we would play with it at Standish's house. We began turning the wagon around right in the middle of the bridge. Like I said, it was crude and hard to handle. Frankie was pushing it and Pearl and I were pulling. The thing was so clumsy and the bridge was just wide enough for a regular wagon to cross. On top of that, the bridge had no sides for protection. During our twisting and turning to get the thing turned around we knocked Frankie halfway off the bridge. She was dangling and trying to hang on the edge of the bridge. We ran to where she was and pushed the wagon out of the way. We tried to catch her but it was too late. Her little fingers couldn't grasp the edge of the bridge any longer. She dropped into pretty deep water. We saw her in that dirty mess. We thought sure she was a goner.

Pearl and I started jumping up and down and screaming for Mama. Mom and Uncle Jessie heard our cry for help and they came out of the house running. They knew something was wrong when they saw only two kids on the bridge. When they reached us, Uncle Jessie vaulted into the rushing water to get Frankie out. He grabbed her before she went under again. Soon as her head was lifted out of the water she started coughing. Uncle Jessie finally made it back up the bank with Frankie in his arms. He handed her to Mom.

Uncle Jessie was completely exhausted from the ordeal he just went through. Frankie looked at Mom and threw her arms around her neck, crying. When we got home, Pearl and I stayed pretty closed to her the rest of the day. I can't recall ever playing with that little log wagon again. We were only four years old at the time. That was one of the most frightening moments in my life.

Chapter 2

Our First Move to the Country

In the late fall of 1927 or early 28 we moved from Palestine to about five miles south of Forrest City. Mom's parents, Jerry and Alice Wilson Smith, left two houses and several acres of land for their eight kids at their death. I don't know why the move. Perhaps it was better pay with another company. So we moved into the larger farmhouse on this property.

I never knew my grandparents. Granddad died the year Frankie and I were born and Grandma the following year. I suppose a person always has empty spots in their lives and one of mine was never having a grandparent to visit each summer. I am glad my grandson, Danny, is old enough to be able to think back on the time spent with his Bo and Nanna. On January 4,1998 my son, Garry and his wife, Lisa, presented me with a birthday present, a beautiful granddaughter, named Shiloh Nikita Edwards. I hope my life expectancy is long enough for her to remember me with fondness.

I don't know how long we stayed at the family home-site. It was constructed of rough lumber that showed its age with many years of Arkansas weather pounding on it. The hallway separated the first two rooms and extended down to the last room. Out of eight siblings in Mom's family, she and Aunt Blanche were the only ones married at that time. Uncle Rodney was the youngest in their family. His bachelor-style furnishings were in the room next to the kitchen. I know, because he caught me peeking at him through a knothole in the kitchen wall just as he started undressing for a bath. He heard me on the other side of the wall and saw my eye looking at him, and too, he may not have known whom the eye belonged to. He came over and stopped the hole up with his sock. Perhaps I was going through a curious stage of my life. No one saw me do this. Nothing was ever said about the incident. I have no idea where the rest of her family resided. They were probably scattered out in the vicinity of our small town.

When we were settled in our country home, Frankie and I took over one of the small empty rooms that joined the chicken house. The room had a dirt floor. We got Uncle Rodney to put in a stove so we could cook and have our little cocoa parties. He was probably around 13 or 14 years old at the time. He found a two-eyed cast iron Ben Franklin stove top that he could use for this purpose. He got his shovel and started digging an oblong hole large enough to fit the stovetop. When everything was just right he put the top over the hole. He put two joints of pipe together to extend up, and then he connected the elbow joint so the smoke would go outside. He gathered kindling and heavier pieces of wood and started our first fire.

Mom gave us a pan and two spoons and our cocoa materials, then we returned to the warmth of our new kitchen to make our hot chocolate. We used a flour sack for our tablecloth on our box table, stuck a wild flower in a pint jar, and set it in the center of our table. We had three china cups and saucers, of which I still have three saucers in my possession, and three of Mom's teaspoons. Our chairs were gallon buckets turned upside down. Uncle Rodney came out and joined us. He made us feel important by gracing our table with his presence. The idea of having our own kitchen made us feel proud.

Every summer our sister, Pearl, would spend a couple of months with Uncle Frank and Aunt Ella Alderson Lawhorn. These are the people that raised my Dad and his sister, Pearl, when Dad's Dad died in Mississippi in 1910. His mother, Leona Littlejohn Alderson, died a year earlier. They both died in their early forties from hard fieldwork. Ella was my granddad's, John J. Alderson, sister. They were always partial to Pearl. This concern could have been due to the untimely death of Dad's sister, Pearl, at the tender age of fourteen. That is probably why my parents named my sister, Pearl.

Mom put Pearl on the bus and sent her to West Memphis for a visit with her favorite Uncle and Aunt the summer of 1928.

When it was time to come home Aunt Ella neatly packed her clothes in a round wicker basket that was about three feet high. When I look back, my mind's eye sees Pearl standing by Mom as she unpacked her clothes and arranged them in her dresser drawer. Frankie and I were standing by the window looking in and watching this procedure. When Mom got about half way down in the basket she immediately sprung back and let out a squeal that you could have heard two miles away. Pearl just fell over laughing. She had gotten this little wooden snake while she was in West Memphis. When Aunt Ella was packing her clothes Pearl dropped her snake in the middle of the basket. The snake looked so real, she knew she had Mom on this one. Mom had to stop right there and regroup her thoughts. That little lady was shook up a bit. She had to figure out if she should spank Pearl or join her in the laughing session. Of course she didn't spank her. I don't recall Frankie and me laughing at this prank, but I'm sure we did. We would never have missed out on a good laugh. Pearl was always somewhat of a prankster throughout her life.

I think Jimmy was born in Forrest City, February 12, 1926 just before we went to Palestine. I just don't remember it. I know Pearl had a first grade book that had a kid in it by the name of Baby Ray. She wanted Mom to name Jimmy, Baby Ray. She and Mom talked it over and they settled on Ray for his middle name. He was named James Ray. That made Pearl proud because she had her a Ray. James Ray has been called Jimmy for many decades now. Jimmy and Johnny are 22 months apart. Jimmy had to be crawling around in the big house somewhere. Maybe Mom did find Jimmy behind a cabbage. I wonder if Jimmy knew where he was born? Daddy must have told him.

I looked up from my writing and saw Jim ambling my way. "Babe, are you through with your rib stitching? I need time out to think about the present," I said as I moved my feet so he could sit beside me.

"Are you making any headway?" he asked in a curious way.

"I think so. Why don't you read what I have written so far? I need to go in the house to refill my glass. Do you want tea or water?" I asked. "Water is fine," he said.

As I returned, I could see him smiling as he read what I had penned.

"Jim, between Palestine and Jimmy's birth is a head scratcher. I can't recall Mom ever saying where her oldest son was born," I said as I leaned back sipping my cool water.

"Little Missy, I've heard you talk about Johnny's birth. That one shouldn't be a problem."

I can't remember Mom's pregnancy, but Johnny's birth is very clear in my mind," I said. "Sit here for a little while and I'll tell you about it."

"I just came out for a smoke, you go ahead and write it down. I'll be back later to read it," he said as he flipped the cigarette butt to the ground and went back to the shop.

One night Dad let us three girls play in our room for an extended length of time. We jumped up and down on the bed. Had a pillow fight, and all the rough stuff that girls do. No one seemed to care or pay any attention to us. We knew we were going to have a baby joining our family soon. Sometime later Dad came in and told us he had something to show us. We jumped off the bed and ran ahead of Daddy right to Mom's bed. We were anxious to see our little red-faced brother. We were three happy girls when we learned that another boy had joined the family on December 21, 1927. Jimmy wasn't two years old at the time so that could be the reason I don't remember seeing him at the birth of John Wilson Alderson. We called him J.W. for years. In his teen years we started calling him Johnny.

I bet anything, that James Ray was born on this same bed twenty-two months earlier, somewhere in Forrest City. Years later, his name was changed to Jimmy.

Mom laughed as she told me the story about Jimmy sneaking Johnny's bottle, because I don't recall this particular event.

Johnny was fed condensed milk that Mom would mix and put in his bottle. When she would give Johnny his bottle she kept noticing that it would get empty mighty fast. She knew Jimmy was always close by when Johnny was fed. One day she gave Johnny his bottle and started walking away pretending not to notice what was about to happen. As she turned around, she saw Jimmy take the bottle out of Johnny's mouth and suck some of the milk out. Then he gave it back to him just before he started crying. Every time Mom would leave, Jimmy would get the bottle and get his share of the milk. Mom started giving Jimmy a bottle as she fed Johnny. Jimmy was just a baby himself.

I didn't help this situation much, either. I loved condensed milk right from the can. Mom would put the can in the cupboard. I would find it and suck most of the milk out of one of the little holes that was in top of the can. Mom kept putting the milk higher and higher in the cupboard.

One day Frankie was helping me with the chair and as I stepped from the chair to the lip of the cupboard I slipped and fell. As she tried to catch me, my face hit the chair.

Mom heard the commotion we made and came to see what was going on. When she came to my aid, I wasn't screaming or crying loud, I was just sitting there whimpering, hoping she wouldn't hear me. Mom came over and hugged me and wiped the stream of tears from my face. She knew what I was doing and how I got hurt. Mom didn't scold me, she knew I was hurt enough just by being caught in the act. She put the chair back where it came from and walked out to another part of the house. Later on that day I did get a swig of milk. Looks like I was a pretty gutsy little kid. I got by that time, but oh, there were other times that I didn't. I can't recall seeing Frankie getting her share of the milk, but I know I wasn't the only one to drain the can.

The last time I made my climb to steal and drain the remainder of the much-loved milk, I was caught red handed. That scared me so bad I liked to have fallen off the ledge I was standing on. I am sure after Mom got through with me; my hinny was red for a week and probably hard for me to forget. That could be why this has stuck in my memory for decades. Frankie had to have gotten some kind of correction. I know I couldn't have been the only little stinker that roamed the rooms of our country home. I was usually the one that would get us in trouble. I know I felt the sting of Mom's hand on my bare hinny when I would deliberately disobey her. I don't know why I was so determine to get the milk. I can still eat it by the spoon full.

Chapter 3

Blackberry Jam

One very hot summer day Mom loaded the boys, a quilt and some gallon buckets in the little red wagon with us three girls bringing up the rear. We were heading for the berry patch. She spread a quilt under the shade of this large oak tree and put Johnny and Jimmy on it. The girl's job was to keep the boys on the quilt. Mom put her belt through the handle of one of the buckets and belted it around her waist and headed for the berries with three extra buckets in hand. We were always in her sight. About an hour later she heard our dog barking and dancing around something mighty close to where we were under the tree. She came out of those briers in nothing flat, berries flying everywhere. She picked up a stick on her way. She knew it was a snake. By that time, the dog had grabbed the snake and was slinging it from side to side. Sometimes he would let go and would grab it again. Us little kids just sat there and watched this performance. Mom thought the dog would throw the snake on us at anytime. She ran up with her weapon, got the dog off that snake and started whopping our enemy good. She finally beat the life out of it and flung it a good ways from us. Mom set down beside the tree to collect her thoughts.

After this little procedure she went back to get the other berries she had picked. She thought two gallons were enough, so we headed back to the house. Mom always transported the boys and the berries in the little country transportation, our little red wagon. She used this method many times in getting to the field and back home. It would take Mom most of the day to pick the berries and make jam. She was pretty tired from the day's work.

This one day after making the jam, she got the boys asleep and told us girls to stay in the house while she took a short nap. When we knew Mom was asleep Frankie and I headed for the kitchen. We got our spoons and a quart jar of unsealed jam and dug in. When we got about halfway down in the jar we heard Mom coming down the hall. We grabbed the jar of jam and stood up under the table. We didn't think she could see us because all we could see were her lower legs and feet. She knew what was going on. We had jam all over us, on the table and the floor. And of course, she saw us. She didn't need to spank us. We ate half a quart of the stuff. Mom gave us a bath and we were put to bed, then she went back and cleaned the kitchen. We ate so much it made us sick. We puked up blackberries for a week. I sure wish I had lost my appetite for sweets at that time. I would probably be a little slimmer today.

I don't remember when we moved back to town. We couldn't have stayed in this old rustic house more than two years before we headed back to the city. I don't know why we moved back.

I noticed Jim standing on the concrete apron in front of his shop. He looked up and saw me motioning for him to come on over. When he arrived, I told him my life story may be worth putting on paper after all. It's kinda fun thinking back on my past life. It seems so long ago.

"Jim, I think I know where Jimmy was born. It was somewhere in town before we moved to Palestine," I said as I sat back in great relief.

"I'm glad you got that settled. I don't know why it bothered you so much. At least you got the kid born. That's all of you kids now, so get on with your story," was his remark as he started to make his way to the house for his evening rest.

"Jim, don't go yet, let me tell you about two more wild experiences I faced in those early years," I said.

I am writing as fast as events come to mind, I laughed to

myself thinking that I should be through with this story before the first snow falls.

"Jim, we moved to a blue, four room, corner house east of town in time for our first year in school. Mom and I were out driving around in Forrest City one day and she said "Annette, stop in front of that blue house there on the corner. This is the house we lived in just before the depression hit." The house was still in very good condition after seventy years. Many funny, sad and happy incidents come to mind when we lived in this spacious structure.

This is the time when Canary, our nanny, appeared in my early memory. I can picture her as a slim person, about 5 feet 3 inches. Canary could make us kids laugh and she would play with us. She helped Mom with housework, cooking, and five kids. I've seen her wash the clothes on a rub-board. A rub-board or washboard is a board having metal ridges on it, used for rubbing the dirt out of clothes. Then she would boil the clothes in a big iron washpot. After that, the clothes were rinsed and hung out on the clothesline to dry. Boy, what a procedure that was. I know. I have worked all day each Saturday with that kind of washing. She also stayed with us when Mom and Dad went out at night.

A fond memory of Jimmy is when Mom and Dad went to a friend's house to play cards one night. Card parties were the main event in those days. She told Canary to put Jimmy to bed at eight o'clock. Johnny was already in bed. Time came for her to get Jimmy ready for bed. When she got the last layer off him he suddenly pulled away from her crying and ran to a corner of the room and stood there buck-naked. Canary asked, "James Ray, what is the matter with you?" She was completely shocked at his reaction.

He said, "Mama told me not to let the girls see me naked." Of course we laughed. Big deal. We've seen him naked many times before. We knew what little naked boys looked like.

Canary finally got his gown on and put to bed. I'm certain this was even funnier when she related the story to Mom.

One night Uncle Jack came by with a huge stalk of bananas. You can imagine how our eyes popped open to see a complete stem of bananas laid before us. They used to hang bananas up in the grocery stores and you pulled off what you wanted. Well, we kids dove in just like a bunch of starved monkeys. Uncle Jack invited Canary to join us. She went outside to the water faucet to wash the snuff out of her mouth. We had a bird dog, Sport, who was our faithful guard, at least that was what Frankie and I thought. Sport heard Canary in the back yard and came after her. Canary raced to the back screen door, and slammed it in Sport's face. Then she started talking softly to him through the screen. Sport knew her and had never bothered her before but he had never seen her spitting and coughing trying to rid herself of that snuff. She finally got her mouth clean and joined us in the banana feast. After we had polished off most of the bananas, Uncle Jack decided to leave the sparsely spaced stalk with us kids.

Sport was a bird dog with scraggly red spots on short dull white hair. Wherever Frankie and I were, Sport was right beside us. No one was loud or acted up in front of our house. If they did, Sport would raise his head, growl, and show his teeth and they would immediately straighten up and walk by very quietly. That was some lovable dog. I don't know what happened to him. I can't recall taking him with us when we made our last move to the country. But he was the one that got the snake at the berry field when we lived in the big house. I know, because I have a picture of Frankie and me with Sport playing in the yard.

There was a family next door that had two boys, Jimmy and Lewis, that were near our age. They would come over and play with us. I can't remember Pearl ever joining in our play, but I know she was somewhere around. My memory of her in these early days just fails me. One day they came over and Lewis and I started fussing about something. Uncle Rodney had left a frog gig in the backyard that he used when he went bull frog hunting. This frog gig had a long wooden handle and on the other end it was metal with three well-sharpened barbed prongs. With that you could just about get your frog every time. We were all barefooted. Louis put his foot somewhere I didn't want it. I told Lewis if he didn't move his foot I would gig it. I clenched the handle of this three-prong weapon, raised it about a foot high, came down fiercely and stabbed his little toe. It amazes me how I had missed the foot and got just one toe.

I suppose Louis has wondered what ever happened to the kid that giggled his little piggy. It would be a rarity if he had no scar. Oh well, I really thought he'd move his foot at the last second. Lewis started crying. Frankie, Jimmy and I joined him in his crying spell. Pearl came out to help. Louis was between Frankie and me, hanging on our shoulders. The way he acted you would think I punched a hole in the foot. We got him home and his mother doctored his toe. I can't recall apologizing. All I did was cry. I still have a picture with all five of us sitting on their porch steps from that day's experience. That was the first and last time I played with the frog gig.

Frankie and I started first grade from this location. We had a friend that lived in a house that adjoined the school grounds. We had a playhouse in the bushes that separated the two properties. That was our secret hideout. We played there every day after our lunch, until the bell rang for us to come in for our afternoon classes.

There was a cute boy by the name of Orlane that came by our house every school day and escorted us to school. Well, I said us, but it was Frankie he walked with and I was jealous of her. Frankie knew I didn't like the attention she was getting. One day she told Mom that she was going to hide her schoolbook and pretend to look for it. She was hoping that would give me a chance to walk to school with Orlane. When he arrived at the front door that day, Frankie told him she had to look for her book and for us to go on and she would catch up when she located it. That didn't work.

He said. "Come on Annette, (my name wasn't changed to Frances until I was in the second grade) let's help her find the book."

Frankie found her book real quick. She and Orlane walked to school and I tagged along in back.

I've thought a lot about what our lives would have been if she had lived.

"Jim, do you think I would still be jealous of her if she had lived? I surely hope not." I said shocked at myself for even thinking of something as horrible as that.

"No, I think you would have gotten over this period of your life. Sounds like both of you were there for each another," he said.

I wish I could recall more of the times we spent together in our earlier life. We did everything together, even at school. I have a school picture of us when we were in the second grade. I remember those sweaters we have on. You can really tell which one is me by the expression I have on my face. I never like my picture made. Why? I don't know.

Chapter **4**

The 1929 Depression

One dreary day with nothing better to do during recess I started throwing rocks up the slide and hit a little classmate as she was coming down at full speed. Why I did this I have long forgotten. The little girl told our teacher, Miss Tatum. Of course, she sent the kid to bring me in. Well, she took Frankie instead of me. When Miss Tatum started shaking Frankie she began crying and wanted to know what she had done. Miss Tatum stopped and said. “You go get your sister.” Well, she did. That day Miss Tatum took all her frustration out on me. I thought she was going to shake my head off.

Jim was still sitting with me while I penned a few more pages. “Little Missy, you pestered me a long time for this swing. You better enjoy it while you can because fall is on its way.”

I handed him my empty glass as he finally got up and headed to the house for his much needed rest. After an hour of rest he came back to join me with a cold iced tea in hand. Seems like you drink a lot in the summertime.

“Jim, I’m glad you brought something cold to drink. I need to get the past years off my mind for awhile,” I said leaning back with glass in hand.

As I stopped for a breather I said, “Babe, this is really going back a long way. Do you want me to write your life story? I’ll bet it would be quite different from mine with your long service record and years of bush flying in Alaska and all over the states.”

“No way,” he said getting up and pretended there was more work that needed to be done on the plane wing.

"Perhaps you are right, I wouldn't want to know your past, at least all of it," I said as I looked up and saw him hightailing it out to the shop.

The depression hit October 29, 1929. Work was getting harder to find. Mom thought we would be further ahead if we moved on some of the property her parents had left her and her siblings. Mom took us out of school and prepared the family for our last move to the country. This time we went to the little house that was further down the road from the one we once lived in. Uncle Rodney and Dad moved the first load of our belongings in the wagon that morning. On their way back they stopped by Mrs. Austin's and had lunch. One of the main dishes was a bowl of souse, better known as headcheese. This was one of their favorite dishes, so they really dug in. By the time they arrived back for the next load they were too sick to even sit up. Mom was shocked when she saw how weak they were as she helped them into the house. Mom sent Frankie and me to get Dr. McCown that lived a block away. We didn't waste any time getting there. We ran. We knew our Dad needed help.

We knocked on the door and an old gray headed man came to the door and leaned over with this horn stuck in his ear. Mom had told us before that Doctor McCown's Dad could only hear a little with this horn. We knew we were to talk into this contraption. By that time the Doctor appeared. We told him Dad was real sick and Mom needed him now. He grabbed his bag and followed us.

By the time we returned home Mom had both men lying on a mattress she had laid on the floor. Of course we kids thought they were dying with all that groaning and moaning. The Doctor said they had ptomaine poison and couldn't be moved that night. They picked up food poison from the souse that Mrs. Austin had served them at lunch. They were well enough to move the next day with help. I never heard if the Austin's contacted ptomaine or not. Surely they did because they ate the same thing Dad and

Uncle Rodney did.

We finally completed our move to the country. How Mom arranged seven people in that small structure is beyond me. But too, you can put a lot of little kids in a small place. I don't know why we didn't go back to the big house. Aunt Blanche and Mom were the only ones married and Mom had five kids. Oh well, we made it and we learned to have a lot of fun in that house with so little space. That next fall when school started we had no bus in our community. Pearl, Frankie and I walked about a mile and a half across the woods to catch the bus on another route. Of course, we had to take our grades over because Mom took us out before we finished the first grade. Frankie and I were eight years old before we got back in school. There were four other kids that made the walk with us five days a week. We would stop by the Fine place once a week to swing on the grape vine with these two cousins. We would swing over a ditch that had a lot of rubbish in it. Frankie and I often thought what would happen if one of us lost our grip and fell into the ditch. We could see one of us landing in a pit of slithering rattlers as big as our arm. Apparently that thought didn't really scare us because once a week we would stop by for another exciting swing.

One day when we headed back home across the woods Pearl and Faye, one of our close neighbors, started fighting, for reasons of their own. Faye had Pearl on the ground pulling her hair and beating her face in. Frankie and I realized Pearl needed help before Faye killed her. I ran up and got me a handful of Faye's sandy red hair and gave it a tug. I backed off to see her reaction. Then Frankie ran up and did the same, only she yanked harder. That got the old girl off our sister. We saw Faye getting up off of Pearl and that girl came after us with fire in her eyes. I tell you, Frankie and I lit out of there as fast as we could. We picked up speed going down the hill. The cows in the pasture stopped eating and looked at us. Every time we would look back, Faye was gaining on us. We finally got to the last barbed wire fence. At last our house was in sight. We dropped to the ground to roll under this prickly wire and Faye caught us. She stood us up and slapped Frankie on both sides of her face. When I grabbed Faye's hand to stop her from hitting Frankie, she got in a blow to my face. Faye had shoulder length sandy hair and that day she looked wild, woolly, and mean. When she turned and started up the road to her house, you could hear her mumbling to herself. By this time Frankie and I were hot, and the sweat made streaks down out dusty faces. In my anger I had to let out a little curse word like, "damn you".

Frankie told Mom that I cursed. Mom had a way of correcting me that would bring tears. She would tell me that was a naughty word and I should never say it again. That worked better than a spanking most of the time. It disturbed us when Pearl didn't come to our rescue. I don't recall ever helping her fight anymore of her battles, either.

We finally passed to the second grade. Later, that grade school was torn down and the grounds were made into a city park. They had built a new high school so the old high school became our grade school.

Dad always had his own sawmill or was the sawyer for someone else. Since we were on farmland, he had plenty of room to set up his mill. I believe from that time on Dad had his own, "Ground Hog," mill. The Ground Hog name was what Dad called his little mill. It was very small, with the bare essentials. Dad put the mill on our property at the back of our house.

It's hard to believe we kids were dumb enough to play in the sawdust pile. That stuff would stick to our sweaty bodies as we played around in it on hot summer days. The thing was we had to pack water to bathe in. One tub of water took care of all five kids. Mom would throw Johnny in last. Johnny has often said he was dirtier when he came out of the tub than when he went in. Talk about the good old days! Some of them were pretty rough. I heard Mom say once that she didn't go to town for seven years. She did have five kids to look after. It's hard to believe that little lady didn't visit her old friends once in a while. Mom loved to get with her town friends and keep up with the latest events. I bet you she did make her appearance in that little town as much as possible.

My name started bothering me. I knew Frankie and Annette weren't twin names. I told Mom to call me Frankie, too. She said she couldn't do that. I wanted Frankie and me to have twin names. Mom got to thinking about names. We sat and talked about this name change for a long time one day.

Mom asked, "How about Frances?" I asked her how it was spelled. She said the last three letters were different. After that I wouldn't answer anyone if they called me Annette. Finally my new name, Frances, stuck.

The next school year Mom took Frankie and me in to register us in the second grade. She signed us in as Frankie and Frances. Mrs. Paterson looked at me and smiled. She knew I had changed my name. That made me feel proud knowing I had reached my first goal in my young life. Frankie and I had our arms wrapped around each other and were giggling when we left her desk, while Mrs. Paterson and Mom continued talking. I went by that name until I signed up for defense work in February 1942, then I had to go by my birth name, Annette Elizabeth Alderson. I needed my birth certificate to work at Fisher Aircraft in Memphis. I knew a lady from Forrest City that worked in this department in Little Rock. When she sent me my birth certificate she had it as Frances Annette Elizabeth Alderson. I never had it changed.

I can see a car driving up. Jim came out of the shop and I squinted to see if it was my friend, Alene, dropping by. I've been looking for her to come by any minute. Jim went to the car to say hello and escort her to the back where I was. The first thing Alene noticed was my swing.

"Hi, come sit by me while Jim gets us something cold to

drink. I'm due for a break," I said putting my pen and pad to the side.

"Annette, I thought we were going shopping. I can see why you didn't arrive this morning. My husband said you called to say you wouldn't be coming. How do you like your swing?" Jim told my husband he was building you one," Alene said as Jim handed her a frosted glass of tea. "What are you writing?" she asked as she squeezed her lemon and gave the tea a quick stir.

"A family story. I'll let you read it when I'm finished, I said.

Jim left us with our gossip as he made his way back to the shop. I am sure glad he has something to do. I would probably go in circles just seeing him around all day, twiddling his fingers with nothing to engage his hands in.

Chapter 5

Our Own Covered Wagon

"Alene, sit back and let me tell you about my covered wagon adventures. I bet you didn't go to school in one, right?" I asked with a mischievous grin.

"Annette you mean a real covered wagon! That makes you sound really old," Alene voiced at the very thought of this primitive transportation.

Mom was the first person to start a bus route in our area. She talked to the other families on Route Two, and convinced them to send their children to school, also. Her brother Edgar, needed a job so he was our first mule skinner.

Uncle Edgar fixed up this wagon and put a tarp over some curved staves and let it drop on both sides to protect us from the cold, damp Arkansas weather that was sure to engulf us as the winter pushed its way in. He put on car wheels to make the trip a little smoother for our journey along our dusty bumpy road. Then he put boards on the sides for our seats and a front seat for himself. The first day of school he hitched up the two mules and we made our way to the highway to meet the school bus.

Uncle Edgar was the hit of Route Two. Every child wanted to ride in our genuine covered wagon, and those that couldn't were green with envy. That winter when we saw our "school bus" rolling to a stop in front of our house, we three girls would leave the house with our hot bricks wrapped in towels. This kept our feet warm on our way to meet the big school bus on the highway. We were the only ones that did this. My days with the covered wagon were most enjoyable. On cold winter days I thought about the people long ago with nothing but a wagon to travel in. How they had to stay under mounds of covers to keep warm as they journeyed to their destination in the cold winter months. We did enjoy going to school in this simple way.

We were always thinking of some kind of mischief we could do as we rode the wagon home. One boy would jump out of the wagon and run along the side where the driver couldn't see him. One day Uncle Edgar caught him as he leaped out the back and made him walk the rest of the way home. The kid grumbled the four miles home but he never did that again. As we grew up this same boy enjoyed thinking he taught me how to kiss. Well, maybe he did.

There were two steep hills on our route just before we got to the highway. On one side of the first hill was the African-American graveyard. I never heard why they moved their graveyard. I know some of it was being washed away, causing this jagged look on the first hill. Maybe they moved their cemetery to the left side where the ground was flatter and away from the hills. Uncle Edgar would always let the mules walk up these steep hills. On the right side of the first hill, there was a bone sticking up out of the ground. We dared Pearl to get it. She couldn't turn down a dare that was as simple as getting that bone. The mules slowed down and Pearl jumped out the back of the wagon. She had to use both hands to loosen the bone enough to pull it out of its deeply rooted space. She made one last tug and yanked the bone from the mound. She was about to catch up with us when Uncle Edgar looked back and saw her with the bone. He tapped the mule's butts with his whip and they started trotting up the hill. Pearl ran faster and faster but couldn't make any headway. She huffed and puffed as she ran behind the wagon. In all of her efforts she was still losing ground. Uncle Edgar made her run up both hills. It didn't matter. At that point in our lives we were young and tough. We walked everywhere we went and this was no problem for her. After awhile he slowed the mules to a walk and she breathlessly caught up with us. We opened the door and she jumped in, completely tuckered out.

When we got home with the bone, we encountered one mad Mama. She didn't like it one bit when she saw what Pearl had in her hand. Pearl stood on the porch holding the bone she had taken from the graveyard. Mom said with a heated voice, "Don't you bring that bone in this house."

That little lady told us whoever the bone belonged to was coming that night to haunt us. Mom gazed up the road. Pearl let out a squeal and spun around to see what she was staring at. You could see a slight smirk on Mom's face. It wasn't past her to pull a trick or so on Pearl, either. As Pearl was looking for a place to put the bone, she thought of the willow tree out in front of our house. She went and anchored the bone in one of the lower forks. We three girls shared one bed, so that night we slept with our heads under the sheet. We were afraid to open our eyes for fear of seeing the ghost the bone belonged to. While we were asleep, I accidentally raked my toenail against Pearl's leg and she vaulted up screaming. That terrified Frankie and me and we sprung up in bed squealing. We thought the bone ghost had Pearl and wouldn't let go. We were three panicky girls. We didn't sleep much that night. The next day as the mules pulled the wagon passed the mound, Pearl tossed the bone back from where it came from.

This is all I can bring to mind about our nine joyous months with our beloved covered wagon. The next year Uncle Edgar converted his truck into a school bus. From that time on we had a bus with a motor that took us all the way to school.

"Alene, I don't think I have told you about our wild journey to pick strawberries. Living in Arkansas, surely you have harvested your share of those sweet rosy berries."

"Yes I have, Annette. This is your story. Tell me what made it so wild," Alene said adjusting herself in her seat.

Our mail carrier, Kinnymen, knew us quite well. He had an old one seater car with a rumble seat. A rumble seat is in the back-end of a one-seater car. This rumble seat had a metal cover that matched the car. All you had to do was lift the lid and the lid became the back of the seat. Now that is the best that I can describe it. The car was getting old and the lid that covered the rumble seat was missing. That left a big hole in the back of the car. I'm sure it was a car that he didn't need any longer. Dad knew he had replaced it with a new one. So we ended up with the car that Mr. Kinnymen no longer needed. We had no transportation, so Dad took the car with open arms.

Mom heard that they needed help in the strawberry fields in Judsonia, Arkansas. The depression was on in full force. Dad wasn't working at the time. My parents, who weren't lazy people, talked it over and decided to undergo this new way of making a little change during this slow period. They would try anything to make a penny for their young family. Uncle Jessie had a two-seater A-Model Ford in his possession. Our wheels was also a Ford. Since Uncle Jessie, Uncle Rodney and Johnny Fine weren't working they decided to go with us.

Early the next morning Mom padded the rumble seat floor with blankets. We three girls were placed on the soft pad and told not to stand up or move about for fear one may fall out. The boys were in the front seat with Mom and Dad. We started out on our journey with the three men following in their A-Model Ford. We didn't get more than ten miles out of town before it started raining. Pearl dug down in one of the food boxes and found the plastic tablecloth Mom had thrown in. This cloth would serve as our protection from the rain. Also, Mom would spread it on the ground to put our food on if that was needed. Mom glanced back through the opening where the glass should have been and saw we had taken care of ourselves so they kept rolling down the dirt road. We encountered many roads of this nature on this adventure.

When the rain finally ceased, Uncle Jessie had his first flat. Everybody bailed out to help patch the tube. They took the wheel off and removed the tire from the wheel. When they pulled the tube out of the tire, it looked like a patchwork quilt because it had so many air holes that were already covered. The men started putting spit on each patch. If it bubbled they knew that was the leaky one. They had a metal kit with patches and glue that was for this purpose. The lid had holes in it to be used to rub harshly over the leak, to prepare it for the glue. At the right time the patch was applied over the leaky hole. They placed the tube back in the cavity of the tire and secured the tire back on the rim. Then they bolted the wheel back on the axle. Now for the pumping job. We girls took the first turn in pumping air into the tube. That didn't last long till Uncle Rodney took over to hasten the job. They filled the tire with the proper tightness to the touch or kick, hoping the thing didn't spring another leak in the process of this crude test. You can imagine how we must have looked vibrating over miles of this muddy, bumpy course. It took us a long time to get nowhere. Uncle Jessie would have one flat after another. Pearl would usually say, "Well, here we go scratch'n and spitt'n again."

We got in gumbo land. Gumbo is gray dirt that hardens after a rain. When that type of soil is wet, it is much worse than ordinary mud. It slowed us down a lot. Night began over-shadowing us. Mom and Dad came to a good spot alongside the road and they parked for the night. A bonfire was prepared. Dad got the box of pots and food out of the back of our car and Mom started preparing our supper. The three men had to prepare their own food. It had stopped raining a few miles back and the stars were out in full force. The campfire was so warm and snugly. We enjoyed the tales the grownups were telling us until we became sleepy and Mom put us to bed in the car. Of course, we girls didn't go to sleep. We could still hear them talking. There was always a deck of cards on hand. They started their Pitch game with a few bets tossed around. That's a game that was very popular back then. They still had their pot of coffee beside the fire to keep hot. Uncle Jessie noticed the fire was dying down so he and Johnny went to the edge of the woods to pick up some fallen tree limbs.

After awhile Dad decided to help them fetch a few sticks. Uncle Jessie was getting the wood and Johnny was holding up lit matches for a little light to see by. You can imagine how much light that put out.

As Dad walked toward them Johnny said, "Jessie, I hear something." Uncle Jessie could see it was Dad, but Johnny couldn't see a thing with that glare in his face. As the match began to burn his fingers he threw it down and ran. With his night vision out of sinc he smacked right into the first tree he came to. As he was going down he yelled out "damn" that penetrated throughout the forest. When he got back on his feet, it was full speed ahead. The road grader had made it's cut along the side of the road and it was half full of water. Johnny hit the middle of the water. He was in and out so fast he didn't get wet. The water did put most of the campfire out.

Dad and Uncle Jessie laughed so hard at Johnny they could hardly make it out of the woods. They managed to bring out enough limbs to keep their fire going. That was also the light for their card game. Mom was curled up on a blanket reading one of her favorite novels.

The next morning after more of the endless flats and the rounds of spitting, scratching and pumping, we arrived at our destination only to find out that the berries would be ready for harvest in two weeks. Mom and Dad thought we should visit Judsonia while we were this close. Judsonia is still known today for it's plentiful crops of strawberries. We scouted around in this town for a while. Dad bought each of us girls a cherry soda. We arranged ourselves in that hole in the back of the Ford, then we began to make our way back home.

Pearl commented with her pop in hand, "I hope they don't have to fix another flat until I get through with my cherry soda. I don't think I can take any more of that spitt'n and scratch'n."

That was a great adventure for us kids. We had never been that far from home. It was years before I really saw a strawberry field and it was in Judsonia after we moved from Anchorage, Alaska back to Arkansas in 1964.

Chapter 6

The Death of My Twin Sister

The first day Frankie and I signed up for the fourth grade she became very sick. Several of us girls were sitting on the back steps of the gym until our buses arrived. Frankie felt so bad she laid her head on Dorothy Nolan's lap. Dorothy and Doris Nolan were twins and were our friends in school. I noticed she didn't look right. She felt warm and was very pink in color. She had no pain but felt so bad she could hardly sit up. When we got home Mom put her to bed and sent Uncle Jack for Doctor McCown. She never got better. Pearl and I knew something bad was wrong with her. Seemed like all we could do was cry. That Friday she died of malaria fever. She had it all summer. Mom and the Doctor thought she was over this illness that seem to plague us each summer. Frankie had the worse case of malaria. I felt like damning the mosquitoes that bit us every day. September 14,1934 I lost the best friend I ever had. I went in and saw her lifeless body. I sat on the side of her bed for the longest time with tears flowing. I finally leaned over and kissed her forehead. I gently patted the tears that fell to her cheeks hoping the dampness would soak in and stay with her on her way to heaven. I went out and joined Pearl under our big oak tree. We held one another sobbing until Mom came out to comfort us. I don't know where Dad was at this time. Knowing my Dad now, I'm sure he wanted to be alone, and too, the boys were probably with him. He had just lost one of his beloved girls. That was the saddest moment of my life. When we buried Frankie in our family plot in the McDaniel's pasture, "September 17,1934" half of me was buried with her.

Life can be cut off so short. Frankie never had the chance to grow up and experience the joy of love, marriage and children. The absence of my sister has been with me to this day. After all, I was left with one half of the egg that made me.

Frankie and I had a pet dove and when she died that dove disappeared and never came back to its roost on the front porch. She probably changed the course of my life. She was easy going. I had a temper. I didn't feel like saying my sneaky word "damn" anymore. This change made a better person out of me, I think. To this day I can't or don't curse. It saddened Frankie when she heard me say naughty things. I have always felt the need for a close friend. I still feel a part of me is missing. At that time my mind blocked out so much that I wish I could recall. I know we did a lot more together than what I have mentioned.

"Alene, does that make any sense?" I asked.

"Yes it does. You hear about these things with twins elsewhere. I'm so sorry. I'll never understand nor feel the pain in your heart. I must go my dearest friend, I'll be thinking about you. I want to read your book when you get it finished."

As she drove away I thought of Frankie. Alene drove around the block and came back.

"Annette, I can't leave you now. My shopping can wait. You have just written a sad part of your young life. I don't want to leave you just yet. I want to hear more."

After her death, school terrified me. For the first time in my life I was completely alone. I was lost. I couldn't get my mind on my books. I would do my homework, but nothing seemed to stick in my head. I had one teacher, Mabel Paterson, that really loved Frankie and me. She was our teacher from the second and third grade and mine through the sixth grade. Maybe Mrs. Paterson had empathy for a little girl alone. I didn't laugh much for the first two years. Seems like I couldn't wash the sadness from my thoughts. I believe Mrs. Paterson detected this in me. She asked me to assist her in painting the border on the blackboard. I would come in at noon and help her with this. I made all A's in her class, which were writing, art and spelling. I gradually made my way out of the sad and frustrated world I was engulfed in.

Before Frankie's death, Mrs. Paterson was forever putting Frankie and me in most of her stage programs. When we were second graders, Mrs. Paterson had us as a Dutch boy and girl in a stage play. This was the largest play we were in. The public was charged admission. I was alone on stage in several programs talking about pictures Mrs. Paterson had hand painted which were projected on a large screen. On the stage, I did my performance with dignity and never faltered. After Frankie's death, I was in one more program on stage. I made my way up in front of the collective body of our grade school to enlighten the kids about two kinds of potatoes. I knew what I was to say. I looked up and saw brother, Jimmy sitting in my balcony seat, or was it Frankie in my momentary vision? Somehow I had forgotten all but the first and last lines of my speech. I said those two lines, then turned and walked off the stage. I have never been before a large body of people alone since then.

I became the world's worst stutterer. I couldn't think straight. My mind would go blank if I were asked to do anything in front of people. I'll never know why this happened to me. I became very shy. That year I flunked the fourth grade. Mom kept me out of school that next school term. She knew I needed timc to get my nerves settled. I stayed with Dad at the mill camp in Pine Tree, Arkansas as long as the mill was there. I made new friends. Across the road from the mill was a one-room country schoolhouse. Two of my new friends would come over at noon for lunch. I would make cocoa for us to share, and then, we would eat our lunch sitting amongst the treetops the loggers had cut down for the logs. These tops had limitless limbs that we would swing and play on each school day at noon. My nerves seemed to be improving. Mom registered me in school the next school term. I was still timid, and I stuttered so badly, you could hardly understand me. Eventually I overcame this affliction that plagued me for so many years after the death of my sister.

When I was in the sixth grade, Uncle Jessie was dating a lady that had a son with beautiful blond wavy hair. Dorothy and I would chase him till he let us catch him, then we would run our fingers through his hair. He was forever trying to remove himself to the furthest corner of the schoolyard, but we knew he enjoyed the friendliness he was getting from two girls.

One day Dorothy and Doris had a fuss with one of the tougher girls. It didn't take much to arouse sixth graders into a fight, and that includes girls, especially when it was two to one. This girl thought she might need help so she told Dorothy to get her girls together and meet them in the back of the schoolyard at high noon Friday. She knew her group of toughies could "way-lay" Dorothy's with one hand tied behind their backs. Well, Dorothy got her squad together. I believe there were about ten of us. We grouped in front of the school and walked courageously to the assigned location that Friday, ready to give'em hell. Dorothy gave us a pep talk on our way. Both teams lined up about five feet apart facing each other with "come on" looks written on our faces.

When it was time to start, we thrust ourselves forward with "murder the scumballs" on our mind. Yelling, "come on you bums." Dorothy and Doris had us all fired up for this all girl battle. We were ready to take them on. Most of us stopped before any "licks" were exchanged. Dorothy and Doris tied into the leader of the other team. Thelma took on two of the toughies all by herself, while the rest of both teams looked on. Dorothy, Doris and Thelma gave the three they tied into a good "licking". When it was all over, Dorothy came to me with hands on her hips and laid into me as if she was ready to take me on and asked, "What is wrong with you, you were suppose to help us!" I told her that I thought she, Doris and Thelma gave the girls a good going over with all that hair pulling and belly punching. Girl, you didn't need me! There should have been a arbitrator on hand. That ended our gang fights.

"I was involved in real stunt action on the school swings. I would sit on the seat while Dorothy and Doris stood up facing each other and they would pump that swing so high we would just about go over the top. Sometimes there would be two girls hanging on the sides, and they would still get the swing so high it was really scary. There were teachers on the grounds standing around talking. They interfered only when a fight arose. It seemed like the six grade boys were forever seeing who was the "head turkey". I don't see how kids go through their young life without getting seriously hurt with the crazy things they do.

Chapter 7

Dad Demands His Pay

By this time all the kids on our route were going to school and every seat on the bus was filled with two or three standing in the isle. The older kids would save seats for their friend or boyfriend to sit beside them. That day I had the only seat left saved for my boyfriend, James. Here comes Pete and flops down beside me. I don't know why we didn't like him. I know I didn't want him sitting by me. I hauled off and slapped him so hard it left my handprint on his face. He immediately raised his hand and whooped me up beside my noggin. My temper kicked in. The boy was a head taller than me and twice as heavy. I don't know where my strength came from but I grabbed him and we hit the aisle. I had him flat on his back on the bus floor and sitting astride him, pounding his face with all I had. Uncle Edgar told us to cut it out back there, but I didn't pay any attention to him. Pete kept yelling in agony and I continued punching in my points. Finally Uncle Edgar came back and pulled me off of him. Poor boy didn't know a girl could whip him. I suppose I put on a good show that day. One of the girls licked her finger and chalked one up for me in mid-air.

"Annette, I must leave now. Call me when you need a sounding board," Alene said, as we walked to her car. "I may get started on my life one day. You make it sound so interesting."

"Thanks for listening to me as I search out certain parts of my life, Alene. You will always have a space here beside me, so hurry on back, you hear," I voiced as she was driving off.

I don't know what happened in the six-grade one day for the whole class to get paddled, except me and James. I was at the blackboard helping Mrs. Paterson when she took one kid at a time to the closet and gave them a swat with her paddle. Whatever happened, I was glad I was up front helping her paint the border on the blackboard. James was just too tall for her to tackle, or maybe he was a good boy that day.

I can see Jim closing the shop door. It's getting late and I haven't started dinner. I know he is hungry. I have been enjoying the mocking bird that is perched in the very top of my maple tree singing his little heart out. I like to think he is doing this for my pleasure. Let's try the new restaurant that just opened," Jim suggested as he headed for the house.

"I'm for that." I said picking up my extra paper and leaving the swing in motion as I left it for the night.

I have cooked and cleaned house most of my life. I told Jim one day that I get "burned" out doing the same things over and over each day. I sure don't mind going out for a meal. So when he mentions going out to eat, I grab my purse and head for the car.

As we sat in silence, waiting for our meal, he noticed that my mind wasn't there.

"How are you doing with your story?" he asked. "You know I grew to hate school. It got worse as the years passed. I still managed to have fun in my own way. I have always looked much younger than my age. Most of my schoolmates never knew I was three or four years older than they were. I bet I didn't weigh eighty pounds in high school," I managed to say as the waitress put our food before us. I looked at Jim and giggled, "I did wonder if their hormones had kicked in like mine."

Jim just looked at me and smiled. We lingered longer than we had intended in the restaurant. We arrived home later than usual. I was tired and ready for bed. I told Jim goodnight, got on the lift and went up for a good night's rest.

Jim has a way of making our morning coffee where the smell floats up to my room through the vent that's about three feet from my bed. I dressed and got on the lift and pushed the down button that I have hit so many times before.

"Morning Missy," Jim said handing me the good rich coffee in my Alaskan cup.

My son, Garry, brought me this several years ago while he was in Anchorage, Alaska on a job and visiting a cousin.

We had our morning discussion over French toast and coffee. Jim went to the Benton airport shop to get the rivets he needed for the plane. I got my paraphernalia in one hand and coffee in the other and headed out to warm the seat of my new swing.

Jimmy and I were always good in our music class. The bandmaster came to test the fifth and sixth graders on their music abilities. We passed the test with flying colors.

He wanted us to join the school band. We told Mom and Dad about what we wanted to do. We knew Mom wanted us to take part in the school band. But with the depression on, we had no extra money for instruments. Dear brother, do you think we could have really made the school band? We'll never know. This could have been an undeveloped talent that got lost in the shuffle. If we were so good why didn't we learn to play our guitar, or the organ Mom had for a number of years? Pearl, Frankie and I would horse around with the beautiful old, antique foot peddled organ. All I could do was pick out a tune with the one finger method.

I was in the fifth grade and had to stay after school for some reason one day. Who knows, I might have made a face at a kid. Sometimes you could be held back for hardly any reason, at least that's a kids thought. Uncle Edgar went off and left me. It was six miles home and I hit the road running. I slowed down going through town and when I got to our country road I started running again. As I came closer to the big hills I had to slow down some. I was getting tired. I can tell you I was scared to pass the graveyard for fear of some unseen something seeing me and would be shaking their fist at me because of what Pearl had done. As I topped the last hill, a couple in a car passed me. As I struggled to get up the bank my feet would slip. When I finally made it to the top I ran as fast as I could until I came to the first house. From there on I felt safe. When I got to Uncle Edgar's house, I stopped by to give him a piece of my mind. I was a small fifth grader ready to face a big man. All he did was give me the money Mom had given him to take me to the circus.

They thought I'd go to Aunt Virgie's house for the night. No, no, not ole Frannie. When I got home I sat on the top steps of the porch and started crying. Mom heard me and came and sat down beside me. She put her arms gently around my shoulders, I turned towards her and sobbed on her shoulder. I said, "Mom, can I go to the circus with Uncle Edgar?" She said, "No, why didn't you stay at Virgies? Don't ever make this walk alone again."

I just sat there and cried in Mom's arms. A kid couldn't walk six miles alone today because it would be too dangerous.

Jim just returned from the airport and I needed to stretch my legs, so I went to the shop to see what he was doing. I don't see how the man can continuously work on those planes. When he finishes one fuselage, he would sell it and buy another one that had been wrecked. Oh well, it gives us our own space. He came to the door just as I walked up.

"Are you getting tired of writing, Little Missy?" he asked as he took the last puff on that cigarette.

"Those things are going to be the death of you," I said as I walked to the shop phone. "I'm going to call Della and see if she'll come over. Alene made it easier yesterday for me to put my thoughts together, so I'm calling Della and see if she will come over and help me get through the next phase of my life."

"Jim, she said she'll be here in twenty minutes and it's almost time for lunch. I'll go in and make a few sandwiches before she gets here," I said hanging up the phone and walking to the house.

I turned the radio on and was humming and dancing with the music when the doorbell rang.

"Della, you didn't waste any time getting here," I said handing her the plate of sandwiches. "I'll bring our drinks."

"Well Annette, you did say you would feed me so let's get with it girl," Della said following me out the door.

"Della, I seem to reminisce better when I have someone in front of me as a sounding board. Do you think you can keep me in line?" I asked as I put the drinks on the makeshift table I had at the side of the swing. Jim joined us for lunch and the first thing he said, "Little Missy, today I will make you a table you can use for writing and serving lunch on."

"That will be great, I do need something to put things on," I said.

When he finished his lunch, he went back to the shop with that on his mind.

"Della, you were in the depression and you know most people had some trying times. I don't know how it was in Indiana where you were raised, but here on the end of Crowley's Ridge, people had it rough. I have always heard that Forrest City was on the tail end of Crowley's Ridge. "Poor" wasn't in my vocabulary at my young age, so I didn't know people were poor. Some of the city kids thought they had more but they didn't. We had a wood burning cookstove and a kerosene lamp, house and land. And all we had was paid for. They had to pay rent, utility bills, and buy food. We raised most of our food and Dad was very seldom without work. We had a good living at one time. Remember Canary, our nanny?"

During the heat of the depression Dad and Uncle Jessie worked for a man (I won't mention his name because he still has folks in Forrest City) that didn't pay them for two months. Uncle Jessie was staying with us at this time. He still had his two-seater A- model they drove to work in. The boss would pay some of the help but not Dad or Uncle Jessie.

"Now think about this Della, Dad was the sawyer and without him no one could work." Dad didn't want to quit because he needed the job.

This particular Saturday morning I heard Dad tell Mom that P-- would pay him and Jessie or he'll go home without a "head" because he would drive it into the ground. Now that was strong words for a man no taller than five feet ten inches. Well, the boss man wasn't any bigger than Dad, so maybe Daddy-O could have "driven his head in" so to speak. There were little kids that were showing signs of hunger. Dad waited for his boss at the edge of town. When he saw Dad he stopped and wanted to know what he wanted. Dad said he wanted his back pay right now and also Jesse's. Of course, he said he didn't have enough to go around. Dad knew that didn't make any sense. He told his boss that if this was a waiting game the other guys can take their turn in line, because he and Jessie had waited long enough.

Today, boss man, belongs to Jessie and me. Dad made him pay every penny due them.

That afternoon we kids were waiting on the porch for them to come home. We saw this A-Model shaking as it came in sight, with the back seat crammed full of groceries. Uncle Jessie backed the car up to the back door. The first thing Dad did was to hand each kid their sack of candy. Dad always had separate sacks of candy for each of us. Then Dad and Uncle Jessie started handing sacks of groceries to us. We stacked all we could on the table. We put the rest on the floor. We stood in awe at the amount of "grub" they brought in that day. We had peanut butter and a loaf of store bought light bread. Back then store bought bread was called "light bread." Now that was enough to excite any kid in their wonder years. What a treat! Uncle Jessie just stood against the car with the most pleasant smile on his face.

From that time on the boss paid Dad and Uncle Jessie every Saturday. Buying groceries wasn't a big deal to Mom and

Dad, because they bought supplies to last two or three months at a time. But when it stretched out to four months or more, that put our cupboards a little empty. Mom always canned several hundred pints and quarts of vegetables, fruits and jelly each year.

My Encounter with a Paddle

"Della, Uncle Jessie did one thing that puzzled me." He had already moved back to the big house. Three of Mom's brothers had their own rooms that they called their bachelors' quarters. Dad and Uncle Jessie rode into town with Uncle Jack one Saturday. Time came when Uncle Jack and Dad were ready to come home and Uncle Jessie was nowhere in sight. They waited and waited. No Jessie. So Dad and Uncle Jack came home without him. About two hours later Uncle Jessie came busting in our front door and wanted to know why they left him in town. Now Uncle Jessie had been drinking and he was really mad. He couldn't fight Uncle Jack because he was crippled in his back so he socked Dad square in his face. Dad wasn't going to just stand there and take it so they tangled. Dad got a lot of good punches in. Mom tried to stop them with no luck. The kids were on the sideline screaming and crying. It seemed to me the fight would never end. Finally it was over. We ran to Dad with arms outstretched, our faces wet with tears. We gave Uncle Jessie plenty of dirty looks and he just stood there with the saddest face. By now he had sobered up to some degree.

He told Mom later that he would never fight my "dad" again. "Your kids taught me a lesson I'll never forget. It might have messed up the love they had for me. That is not a good thought for me to live with." I went to see my Aunt that lived in the same house one day right after the fight. As I was leaving I looked back and saw Uncle Jessie standing at the window looking at me. We held up our hands and waved at each other. I'll never forget the look on his face. That made me love him more.

"Della, did I tell you that I stood in the middle of Mrs. McDanials office with a paddle aimed at my butt when I was in the six grade?" I asked, as I rearranged my pillow I had for my back. "No, tell me, this must be a goodie." she said.

Everyone that brought their lunch to school had to eat it in the auditorium. We sat two to a seat. That day Thelma and I shared this front row seat. This was during the depression. If you had light bread for sandwiches you were lucky. This time we both did. Thelma had a peanut butter sandwich and I think I had cheese. I gave her half of mine for half of hers. What a mistake. Thelma started in on her peanut butter sandwich. She started showing signs of choking. By that time I took a bite of mine. The sandwich was so dry you could hardly swallow what you chewed.

She barely got out, "Frances, let's get some water." I said, "Okay, you go first."

We were down front, right by the door that lead to the gym. Miss Johnson was on the other side of the room playing the piano, so out she darted and I followed. After we got our drink we started sneaking back in. While we were out, Mary told the teacher what we had done. We weren't seated good when we saw this tall, skinny teacher coming toward us. She dismissed the kids and took Thelma and me to the office. She got the paddle out and started toward Thelma. Thelma backed up so she grabbed me. She told me to bend over. Now we were six graders. I did a half bend and she whooped my behind two times. I started straightening up a tad and she stopped. I guess she thought we were going to scream and cut up. We didn't shed a tear. When she got through with me, she grabbed Thelma before she could back off. She told her to bend over. After one lick Thelma raised up and they looked eyeball to eyeball and that was the end of that. She told us to never sneak out again behind her back while she was playing her music. I wonder what would have happened if we really jumped up and down and screamed really loud. Miss Johnson would have probably lost all composure right there. She might have thought we were going to turn on her and give her a whipping.

There was a long cloakroom where the higher grades hung their coats and put their lunches. Miss Johnson had hall duty that day. She put me on one side of her and Thelma on the other side. That meant no playing at noon. We saw Dorothy and Doris come in and go the cloakroom. Thelma and I slid down to the two openings and I felt a hand hit my side. I stuck my hand around toward her and Dorothy gave me a hand full of candy that she had broken into little pieces. I put the candy in my pocket. Doris did the same for Thelma. I know this was sneaky but Miss Johnson never knew we were eating candy.

The next day we met the bus that Mary was on. When she got off the bus, Thelma and I got her between us. Not knowing what we would do to her, she became pretty nervous. Thelma told her if she ever told on anyone else that she would whip her all over the school ground. Thelma looked at me and said, "Won't we Frances?" I said, "Yes, we sure will, you little tattle tale." I could talk big with Thelma around. She was a strong little tomboy.

"Della, this may be a little hard to believe, and maybe not. You know me quite well," I said as she looked at me with a quizzical look.

Okay, you know how you try to be honest, then things happen where you can really rat on a person. My brothers would play hooky from school every so often. They would give me a nickel not to tell Mom. Then they would give me a nickel to write an excuse to give the teacher. Of course I'd take the money and give them my solemn promise not to tell Mom. Sometimes they would make me so mad that I would tell Mom what they did. That was pretty good leverage to hold over their ornery heads. As soon as they found out that I squealed on them, I knew my name was mud if they ever caught me. I would make myself scarce until Mom came in from work. They wanted their nickel back. By then I had already spent it on candy at school. "You know, Della, when we are together now we can have some good laughs about what happened long ago in the hills that we named "Chigger Ridge" because of the millions of chiggers we'd get in the berry fields."

"What kind of pests did you guys have in Indiana?" I asked.

"Fleas that our dog would bring in the house. Stop it Annette," said Della. "You make me itch."

"Della, I can tell you a lot of things that happened in the thirties."

Mom went on a trip to Little Rock, Arkansas with a group of ladies for a week. Mary Powers, one of our older friends, would stay with us in the daytime while Dad was at work. Uncle Edgar came by our house one day with a sled of watermelons. He gave each of us one. Johnny, Jimmy and I thought we got cheated because our melons weren't ripe enough. We got our sled and went down the hill to his melon patch. We put all the melons the sled would carry, which was three. The sled pulled pretty smooth until we got to the hill. I was behind pushing and the boys pulling. "Della, I suppose you have never tried pushing a sled up hill, right?"

Well, we got about halfway up the hill and we heard this voice saying, "You stole my melon, you'll never go to heaven." We stopped right there and took note on what was ahead. It became quiet once again so we started pushing and pulling that dumb sled once more. The voice sounded again and came in louder with stronger force. We stopped. It was getting a little spooky on the hillside. We didn't know whether to run back down the hill or try to make it up the hill and leave our melons behind. As we were trying to decide what to do, we looked up the trail and saw a limb shaking with something white perched on the limb. As we walked closer, we heard someone laughing so hard she nearly fell out of the tree. It was Pearl with a sheet over her, exercising another one of her pranks. Mary was anxiously waiting at the top of the hill to hear all of the details. Mary didn't want to spoil Pearl's fun, so she stayed out of sight. The melons we got were no better than the ones that were given us.

Pearl and I did a lot of things together, like going to parties and our Wednesday night prayer meetings. I would shoot marbles with my brothers and climb trees with them. Pearl and I liked to party together. Of course we had to walk everyplace we went. The young people our age would group together to go places. That was always a good time to hold hands with our boyfriends. We would go to the Tynes house and play poker with a deaf teenager that became deaf when the doctor gave him a shot in the spine. He had a sickness that this was supposed to have helped. But it didn't. We went swimming in a pond called Traps Pond. I was always afraid a snake would wrap around my leg, but we never saw a snake there. There was an apple orchard near by that we would raid during apple season. It was a big orchard so we thought they wouldn't miss a few apples. Oh well, we enjoyed ourselves.

We had to make up our own games to play or do things to entertain ourselves. One of them was playing in a big pile of leaves. "Della, how does a mountain of leaves grab you?"

Pearl and I piled up a large amount of leaves under a big tree limb that hung out over this low spot in our grove. Then we would climb the tree, get out on the limb and make our way over to the top of the pile of leaves, then drop off. It was always a soft landing. On one of the drops, I didn't land just right and it knocked the breath out of me. There I lay, all doubled over and couldn't move. I motioned for Pearl but she thought I was trying to trick her in some way.

She said, "You better move or I'll drop on you."

I finally rose from the leaves and she saw I was in trouble. She dropped out of that tree in nothing flat, grabbed me and started screaming for Mom. Mom shifted in high and was out of the house on a run. Anytime she heard a scream she knew it was serious business. Mom started slapping me on the back. I was already turning blue. She finally knocked some wind in me. I don't think there is any pain worse than a thousand needles sticking your lungs. I don't know why Pearl played in the leaves with me. It was her suggestion. This is the only time I can recall Pearl ever playing in the leaves with me. She would join us when we would go to the woods and swing on our favorite grapevine. She had a friend about a mile down the road she chummed with.

"Della, I'll tell you another incident that happened as night was pushing it's way over us."

Pearl and I had the ironing board set up on the backs of two chairs under our big maple tree. Dad bought Mom a new wood cook stove and they had set the old one in the back yard for Mom to can and cook on in the summer. We heated our irons on this setup. We had ironed all day. Mom went in to cook dinner while we stayed outside.

After a long wait Mom called out to us and said, "You kids lock the smoke house and come in, dinner is ready."

Pearl said, "The last one in has to lock the smoke house." She made a dive for the back door. I got up to run and I hit that ironing board at full speed. I got the breath knocked out of me again. I hit the ground as I grabbed my painful chest. No one knew I was in trouble. I tumbled around on the ground for a few minutes. My lungs began to take in some air. I finally got up and went in and sat down at the table. I was still pale and Mom wanted to know what was wrong. I told her I ran into the ironing board and it knocked the breath out of me. She made the other three kids go back and lock the smokehouse.

"Della, let's have another glass of tea. I'll tell you about our pie and box suppers we had three or four times a year at our church when it needed more operating expenses." "Hey girl, am I putting you to sleep?" I asked waiting for her response.

"No, no, I'm trying to place myself into your events. I think I would have enjoyed being there with you," Della said as she repositioned herself in her seat.

We would have pie suppers that were held at the community hall. This place joined two communities, the Powers and the Smith. We girls would always tell our boyfriends which pie or box was ours. We just didn't want old men buying what we brought, because you had to eat with the person who bought your pie or box. No one was to know whose box belonged to which lady. Every box and pie was sold to the highest bidder. Very seldom did we ever have to eat with someone old enough to be our daddy.

"Della, we did a lot in this era of the thirties. I know some things weren't right, but we did it. We weren't to conscious of some of the things we did because we didn't think God would zap us if we took a few melons. We went to church every Sunday. We thought we were a pretty good group of young people.

After our prayer meeting one Wednesday night, the kids (we were all teenagers) from both communities stood around outside the church until Mr. Cobb, our minister, and Mr. Raglan, our deacon, left the grounds. One farmer said if he caught anyone in his melon patch, he'd shoot them. We didn't believe him. He just wouldn't shoot kids. About fifteen of us young people headed for this gun toting man's melon patch. When we got to the melon patch, the boys went in and picked out the best they could find. Then they brought the melons to the fence and handed them over to the girls. The moon was shinning so bright that night. We ate our melons in the shadows of the trees so no one could see us. Now wasn't that sneaky. We ate the hearts out and left the rest. The next day, we heard about this terrible thing someone did to this man's melon patch. Mr. Todd was so mad he was ready to whip everybody. He never knew who raided his prize melon patch. Some of these young people were his nearest neighbors.

When Mom heard about this she asked, “What a shame, were you girls in on this?”

All we did was look at Mom and Pearl said, “Hum, did they really? Oh, that is a shame. Poor man, I bet he won’t go around bragging about shooting people caught raiding his melons again.”Mom didn’t push us, but I bet you deep down she knew we had our rightful place in this sneaky group of young churchgoers.

“Della, when the moon was the brightest James, the Jackson girls, my brothers and I would go on our possum hunts. The only time I can recall getting a possum was if Uncle Edgar went with us. He always kept the hide and gave me the possum.

He sold the hide for twenty-five cents. The manufacturers made coats or whatever out of different hides they would get. I’d take the possum home and Mom would bake it with sweet potatoes for Dad and me. We were the only ones that would eat the possum. Most of the time we would build a bonfire in the woods and sit around and talk till midnight.

We always had something going in the summer months. We’d get Uncle Edgar to take us fishing or to the football games during school. He did have the largest transportation in our community. His school bus held a lot of people.

“You know Della, he always pulled this Tom Sawyer stuff on us. Or was that Huck Finn?” He’d tell us he had to get his corn or cotton hoed out before he could do anything else. About five or six of us would get our hoe’s and head for his field. He knew how to get freebies out of us.

James was enjoying lunch with us one noon and we were talking about cotton and other hoeing jobs that only the field can produce. I thought I’d get in on some of these intelligent conversations. I piped up and said, “You know Mom said she was the best hoer in her family." I didn't realize how that sounded until she liked to have knock my leg off. I was sitting next to her. I looked at her and she gave me one of those dirty looks only a mama can give when a kid has done something wrong. We left Mom with the dishes and we went outside and had a good laugh.

Not long after that incident, James was back at our house and I thought I'd show off a bit and prepare lunch for my two brothers, James and myself. I don't know what I had but it wasn't much. I fired up the cookstove and proceeded to make some biscuits. I got the table set and food on and we "bellied up" for a nice feed. I passed the biscuits around and everybody took one. I noticed my brothers gathering more than one and putting them in their pockets. I had good teeth and I couldn't get one bite off. They were the hardest things I ever made. I looked out the window a little later and the boys were in a three-handed ball game, using my biscuits for their ball. They would bat those hardtacks and they wouldn't pop open. I still hear about the hardtacks I made that warm summer day.

In the summer months, the young people held a party at one of our houses most every week. We had a "tacky" dress party one night at a neighbor's house and Mom dressed up as a little old woman. She had saved one of her mother's old dresses and a hat from the late 1800's. She put the black dress on that came down to her feet. Cocked the hat on her head, got her walking stick and headed out to the party. As she was walking up in the yard someone asked, "I wonder who that is?"

As she drew closer to the crowd, someone turned the record player on and as the music started, couples began to dance. Mom propped her walking stick against a tree, grabbed herself a partner, and danced till the party ended. Mom won the prize that night. I don't know if they gave a prize or just a recognition. They would always be surprised if Mom showed up at these tacky parties.

"Della, Uncle Rodney was the only one of my uncles that bought new cars back then." This one time he brought home the latest Chevrolet. I was about thirteen during this time. Nola, a friend that was grown, who later became my aunt, and I went out to check it out. She sat under the wheel for awhile then I took my turn. After a fling with the wheel I returned to the passengers seat. Nola said, "Frances, I wonder what kind of car this is?" I looked on the glove compartment door and saw a name. I said, "It's a Chev-o- let." I pronounced it just like it showed in print. That satisfied her. I thought I was really something pronouncing a word like that.

"Della, you can always look back and see silly things in your life you can laugh about."

Chapter 9

JIMMY'S TRICK FAILS

I took my kids to see how sorghum molasses was made once as we were headed for Searcy, Arkansas. They thought it was an interesting procedure. I told them that when I was a kid, I helped Uncle Dorris, one of our older African-American neighbors, as he made our molasses. I helped run the cane through this compressor that extracted juice from the cane. Quite often I would get on the donkey and go round and round as he turned the press. The contraption Uncle Dorris had to cook in was about ten feet long and maybe four feet wide. He had several partitions in this ten by four metal frame. At the end of each partition there was a hole. He had a hotter fire at the beginning and it tapered off as it went to the other end of this cooking unit. He would pour the fresh juice in the first partition and it would start cooking.

He had a wooden handle that had a metal piece that looked like a hoe on one end, that he would use to stir the juice with. When it cooked for so long, he would open one of the holes in the partition and let the syrup flow to the next unit to cook. He would then pour fresh juice in the beginning unit to start the process over. The juice cooked in each unit a certain length of time, then he would open a hole for it to flow to the next unit. By the time it reached the last unit it was ready to pour in our gallon buckets. When the first batch of molasses was finished on the far end, Uncle Dorris would dip the spoons that he formed from the cane into the molasses and handed each kid a big taste of the sweet molasses. We had enough molasses to last a year. If some of it went to sugar, Mom would heat the bucket of syrup in boiling water until it became syrupy again. Some of these depression years were interesting but most were simply the pits for me.

"Della, we did have a few scary moments growing up on "Chigger Ridge."

My siblings and I had been playing all afternoon at a neighbor's house about a mile away. We were supposed to be home before dark. We weren't home so Mom started her journey to get us. Uncle Floyd lived a little past our friend's house, so Jimmy went to see him. In the process he traded a tire for something, I don't recall what, but he got the short end of the stick. By that time Mom met us and wanted to know where Jimmy was. It was getting pretty dark and finally Jimmy appeared. Mom learned what had happened. She told us three to go on home. She took Jimmy back to get the tire. When we got to the house the back door was open. Pearl looked at me and said, "Let's make Johnny go in first." Johnny turned to run and we grabbed him. We took him to the door entrance and bodily threw that kid into the kitchen. He landed in the middle of the floor kicking and squealing. We heard movement on the front porch and we took off running back down the road. Johnny picked himself up off the floor and shot out the back door and passed us in nothing flat. When we got out on the road we heard this hoot owl yelled out 'whoo whoo' in a tree overhead. Pearl said, "I didn't hear that". We shifted in high gear and we were gone. No kidding, with this amount of speed built up in our little bodies we passed Mom and Jimmy.

Mom yelled out, "Where are you kids going?"

We stopped and turned around and joined our family and we preceded our trek to the house. The noise we heard back at the house was two of our neighbors waiting on the front porch for our return home.

Della said, "Annette, I'm going to have Betty and Alene meet me here tomorrow. They do enjoy your stories. One thing I can't do is remember many things that far back."

"Della, when you start thinking about your childhood I bet you would be surprised at the things you can come up with, especially if you have your sister around," I said shifting in my seat. "Can you recall the last time your butt met the strap? I can."

Jimmy and Johnny tore into each other one day and I thought one would kill the other. I was thinking, boy, don't do the killing part yet. Let's grow up more. I jumped off the daybed and tried to separate the two. Those suckers turned on me. The three of us went round and round for awhile. I thought I'd better get out of this before I got whipped, so I went back and took my former position on the daybed. After five minutes or so they were still going at each other. I jumped in once more and tried to separate the two. I still came out a loser, so I returned to my throne. When Dad was working you could hear the mill running. I heard the mill shut down and I knew he would be in soon. I told the boys Dad was coming in, but they still wanted to beat each other's head in. I saw Dad enter the kitchen and get his razor strap. He stood in the doorway watching all of this until the boys saw him.

Dad said, "Okay boys, you first Jimmy." Dad tied into him, then it was Johnny's turn. Dad got Johnny's arm and they went around and around. Johnny could yell louder than any kid I've ever known. Dad saw Jimmy peeking from behind the door laughing at Johnny. He let Johnny go and grabbed Jimmy again. I thought sure Dad was going to kill the boy. Of course, he wasn't but that is a kid's thinking. I jumped up off the daybed, made my way into the ring and grabbed the strap. I told him that was enough. Dad saw what was happening and as he got control of the strap I jumped out of the ring, but not before I felt the sting of his strap on my butt. I was sixteen at the time.

"Della, this is another time in our past that my brothers laugh about when we are together. That was the last time I made my services available".

I saved Johnny from getting shot by Jimmy's fiery temper once.

"What happened that made Jimmy so mad?" Della asked shifting in her seat.

A little bird got in the house and both boys were trying to catch it. Jimmy got it first and Johnny was trying to take it away from Jimmy. During the process, Johnny grabbed the bird and somehow it got away and flew off. That made Jimmy real mad, so Johnny ran. Jimmy caught him in the yard and they had a good fight. Jimmy made the remark that he would shoot him. So he ran to get the rifle. As he ran back in the house to get the rifle, I was right behind him. He beat me in the house, but as he was coming out I took the rifle away from him. We talked until he cooled off a bit. I put the rifle back in its rightful corner. I bet Johnny was glad I was there to defend him. I wonder if Jimmy really would have put a bullet in Johnny's butt like he said he was going to. I doubt it. And too, maybe he would have been so far down the road he would have completely missed his target.

"Della, Mom had to work." This was the depression and there were six mouths to feed. She didn't know everything that went on at the house. She was six miles away working and Dad was about three miles across the woods at the mill most of the time. Many times he would move his mill where the timber was. You had to walk to wherever you went. After a hard days work no one felt like walking three to five miles home. Many times the mill hands and sometimes Dad would set up camp and go home on weekends. I can hear Dad now talk about the time when he was a young boy helping his Mom make yarn on their spinning wheel. He told me once he would build me a spinning wheel, but never got around to it. It really fascinated me how you could take sheep hair and make thread.

"Della, in our day and in our own time we managed to learn a lot, didn't we? I don't know if I should tell you all of this stuff or not. It could get pretty boring. We really had a lot going for us in the thirties, or should I say, experienced a lot." I told you we had a big blackberry patch. My brothers and I thought we would go to the berry field and pick enough berries to make a quart of wine. Jimmy went ahead of Johnny and me. When Johnny and I started approaching the berries we heard someone talking and the briars shaking. The voice said, "Come over here Robert, there's plenty of berries." Johnny and I stopped right in our tracks. I told him to stay here while I get Dad. I took off running toward the house. I met Mr. Ambrose on the road. I passed him like a bullet. He asked, "What's your hurry?" I said, "Nothing," and kept running. I didn't want Robert to know he was caught stealing our berries. When I reached the house, Dad was in the grove helping a neighbor sew his mattress. I'll tell more about the mattress making later. As I pulled Dad toward me, I told him what was going on in our berry patch. He stuck his needle in the mattress and we took off to the field. When we arrived on the hill overlooking the berries, Dad told me to go to the back side of the field and see if Robert escaped in that direction. I did. Dad joined Johnny on the slope. He asked Johnny where Robert was hiding. Johnny pointed in the direction of the voice. Jimmy realized the jig was up for him, so he really put on a show. He started shaking the briers and talking to "Robert." Dad and Johnny ran down the hill and Dad said, "Okay, Robert come on out, I got you."

I heard all of this and I couldn't stand it any longer. I went through the brier patch on this little skinny trail and got scratched from head to foot. I looked down just in time to see a chicken snake in my path. I had the full force of running pushing me on. I couldn't stretch out my stride enough to miss that snake. I got him about four inches behind its head. I was on and off that snake before it had time to grab me. I tell you I was some scared kid. I kept going for fear I'd miss this big event. I reached them in seconds and found out what happened. Dad was waiting on Robert to come out, when Jimmy finally exposed himself and stood there with a smirk on his face. Johnny laughed so hard he could hardly stand. Dad didn't know if he should beat the tar out of that boy or join in on this practical joke. I do believe Jimmy got a lick or two. Couldn't have been much. Jimmy didn't know I would go get Dad.

"Della, just visualize three little kids heading out to pick a few berries to make a quart of fermented juice." We thought all you had to do was to extract the juice from the berries and add sugar. We did that, then we put the juice in a quart jar and covered the opening with a cloth. We took this prize jar of juice to the edge of the woods and set it in a hollow stump to ferment.

We didn't want anyone knowing about our wine making for fear they would seize our concoction and drink it, and we would never know what it tasted like. We decided three days was enough time for the juice to ferment, so we went to check it out. We lifted it very gently out of the stump, removed the cloth and started sampling our makings. We didn't know how a person feels when they consumed a quart of wine. We stayed at the edge of the woods for awhile and just acted silly.

"Della, the juice tasted pretty good. I was a little thirteen-year-old kid and Jimmy, ten and a half and Johnny eight and a half. How do you like that for three little wine makers."

"Like I said Della, my brothers and I can look back on those days and still have a few side splitters."

We had one of the largest "pound" suppers and dance those hills ever had. I believe I can rightfully say that extends to this day and we left those hills in 1942. We always held dances at our house. Mom was what you might call a dancing fool. She did love to dance. All Dad would do is the Buck Dance. Mom invited our two communities to this event. The town folks that knew Mom invited themselves to this dance. Mom lived in this area so long that she knew most everyone. And it looked like they all came. We had a victrola, the kind you wind up. A cousin, Burt Cornelious, brought his guitar and French harp. People came from all directions. By ten o'clock p.m., our kitchen table was overflowing with food. Most brought more than a pound of food. The living room was so full of people you could hardly dance. Burt picked up his guitar and harp and half of the people followed him to the grove. We had lanterns hanging off two or three tree limbs to lighten up the yard. People still came. They danced more than they ate. There was so much food left. Around three that morning, people started thinning out. Of course they went in all directions. Della, some even took out across the woods which was a short cut home for many. Mom made a Lady Baltimore cake for this event.

Mom and Dad came out of Alaska in 1962 to Salem, Oregon to see if that is where they would go to retire. Jimmy wanted Dad to teach him the mill business, so they moved back to Forrest City, where Mom and all of her siblings were born. Her Mom and Dad lived here in the late 1800's. Mom told me her Mom and Dad came over by boat on the Arkansas river. She showed me where they got off the boat. Some of her Dad's people lived in Nashville, Tennessee, so that could be where they originated. I have no idea why her folks came to Forrest City. South of Forrest City is where all the kids were born. She was very much attached to this area. Her Mom and Dad and most of her brothers, one sister and Frankie are buried there in our family cemetery on the McDanials property. Now my Mom and Dad are there.

While in town one day who would she run into but none other than one of the men that had invited himself to the dance she had given so many years back. He thought she was dead. He was shocked to learn that she and Dad had retired in Alaska before they moved back to more familiar grounds. He gave her a big hug and told her that was the best cake he has ever eaten. "Katie, what kind of cake was that you made?" he asked. Mom told him it was a Lady Baltimore cake. Now don't count on the spelling, because the recipe is so old, it may not be around anymore. He told her that he and his wife have never been to a dance equal to the one she gave back in the middle 30's.

"Della, Frankie and I were baptized and became members of the Presbyterian Church at age ten. The minister's name was Graham and he smoked cigars. Well, I thought if he smoked why can't I. Must not be all that much wrong with it. So, in my middle twenties smoking became one of my worst habits. By the way Della, remember Fred Graham, the journalist that was with the news on one of the networks a few years back? Our minister was his daddy. I have been in his house and played with him and his toys."

As kids, Jimmy and I would sneak out and smoke every chance we got. I remember when I got two cigarette papers, then waited for my chance to hit Dad's tobacco can. That night I caught Dad in the kitchen and I got enough tobacco for two smokes. I motioned for Jimmy, and we headed for the back of the chicken house. We rolled the mess up neatly and struck our match and started puffing away. Next thing we heard was Dad's voice, "Okay, you kids, I got you, come on out."

We knew he needed evidence so we stomped the remainders in the ground. Dad didn't whip us but Uncle Jessie was sitting in the kitchen doorway as I walked up. It really was humiliating to me knowing he knew what happened. But too, it was easy for me to be embarrassed.

"Della, Jimmy and I wondered why Pearl followed us to the back of the hen house and then went and told Dad what we were doing. As much as that girl did! We never told Mom the things she did that wasn't right." Jimmy said, "The old booger man is going to get her one day."

Chapter 10

WE IMPROVE OUR COUNTRY LIVING

"Della, a lot of things that Pearl and I did together, we didn't want Jimmy and Johnny along. We thought they were too young for our crowd. We went places that we didn't want the jug heads with us. We had our special boyfriends we wanted to be with.

After church one Sunday all of the young people gathered in Harding Smith's pasture to play ball. There were enough guys for two teams and just about as many gals. The girls yelled for their own team. I'd yell out, "James, knock that sucker in the next pasture." When the game was over, we gathered to decide what to do next. It was getting close to dark. Pearl suggested that we could have a chicken fry at our house. This was around 1936, and that year we did have a lot of chickens. We didn't even think about what Mom would think about this chicken feast. When we got home and told her what we wanted to do, she was all for it.

The boys caught and dressed out about ten chickens, while some fetched wood and started a fire in the outside cookstove. The girls started frying the chickens. Mom was in the house making biscuits. All we had was chicken, gravy and biscuits. Mom couldn't imagine what was happening to her biscuits. She would bake two large pans of them at a time till golden brown and bring us two plates of them steaming hot. When she returned to the kitchen to put the next batch in the oven and bring the rest out to us, there were hardly any left. She knew we didn't come in to get them. Something strange was going on. The boys were in the next room and appeared to be asleep. This was an uncanny puzzle for Mom to sort out. She kept making bread and they seemed to vanish into thin air. For some reason, Mom wouldn't let Jimmy and Johnny join in our cookout. She made them stay in the house. Of course, that made them mad. They were too young to join our group of teenagers. Everybody had a ball that night. Pearl and I were the only ones ever to give a chicken cookout for the young people in the two communities, and I can pretty well say till this day on this one, also.

The next morning, Mom and Dad went to work. Pearl and I started making beds and giving the house a quick straightening up before we started our other chores. Would you believe we found biscuits in the pillowcases, behind pictures, in drawers and under the mattress? You name it and you would find biscuits. When Mom came in from work that evening we told her what had happened to her bread. I think she made the boys eat some of them with their dinner that night.

"Della, have you ever tried sneaking into your house with shoes in hand and be caught red handed? Pearl and I did once."

Gene Ambrose told Mom if she would let Pearl and me go to this party at a friend's house in the Powers community, he would have us back by midnight. Mom asked, "Gene are you sure you will have my girls back here by midnight?" He gave his solemn promise. There were Gene and Virgie, Pearl and Ed, and James and me. Gene came by and picked us up. Now it was a one-seater car. Gene, Virgie and Ed were in the seat and Pearl sat on Ed's lap. James was on the left fender and I was hanging on the right fender. We did our flirting by holding hands over the top of the car. Back in those days the cars weren't all that wide. We got to the party in good shape. We always had fun at these outings. About eleven thirty Gene said, "Pearl, I better get you and Frances back home." We told every one goodnight, took our positions in and on the car and headed for home, or so we thought. There was a beer hall at the crossroads on our way home. Gene pulled in and told us he won't be long. We waited and waited. It was past twelve. Pearl and I got nervous. This was a small beer hall. This joint had windows in it and we saw Gene sitting at this table with other people. Virgie and Pearl went and knocked on the window. Gene saw them and made a motion that he would be right out. They came back to the car. Thirty minutes passed. They went back to the window once again and told him we had to get home. That time he came out, got in the car and we headed home.

Before we got to the house Pearl told Gene to cut the engine off and we pushed the car to our house. They didn't start the car up until they were well past our house. Pearl and I took our shoes off before we reached the porch. We started tiptoeing in and just as we got in the doorway Mom said, "I'll see you girls in the morning." We liked to have jumped out of our skin. It was a dark night and you walk into a dark house and something like that whispers in your ear. "Della, I'm afraid that would have made you a little jumpy too, right?"

That Sunday morning Pearl and I stayed in bed as long as we could. We didn't want to face an angry Mom. I bet we weren't up ten minutes until a car drove up in front of the house. Gene, Virgie, Ed and James got out and came in. The first thing Gene said was, "Katie, it was my fault the girls came in late. I'm sorry." Every one was agreeing. We had a small breakfast together and they went home. Deep down she knew it was Gene's fault that we were late. Mom forgave him, but we never went anyplace with him again.

"Annette, I must leave, it's getting late. I've enjoyed being your sounding board for the day. If you don't mind Bettie and Alene will meet me here tomorrow. I see Jim closing the shop door. I bet he's getting hungry. Have you thought about dinner?" Della asked as she got up to leave.

"I have stew made, maybe he'll settle for that. I also made his favorite pecan pie," I said getting up and walking her to the car. "See you tomorrow. Boy, this has been a long day."

Jim and I walked into the house together. He put his arm around my shoulders and wanted to know the progress I was making.

"Jim, I believe I can complete this as long as I have someone to tell my past to. I'm glad Della, Alene and Bettie will be here tomorrow. I can at least get myself out of those hills and in defense work. It's amazing how much happened from 1935 to 1940."

"Jim, a year or so after Frankie's death my life took off on a new start. I will always feel incomplete because of the absence of her presence in my life. I know God puts nothing before me that I can't handle, but this has been a big one to deal with all my life," I said stirring the stew pot.

"Little Missy, you look tired. You get a program on TV and I'll serve you."

"Thanks, I sure wish you could cook. I have always said that if I could afford a cook, it would be a good-looking Frenchman, at least for one meal a day."

"Jim, you were led to believe you were half German. At your mother's, the Byssee family reunion, you found out you were French. All these years you thought you were a hotheaded kraut. Now do you mind turning yourself around and being this lovable, butt pinching Frenchman? Man, what a change that would be." I said as he handed me a bowl of stew and crackers.

I ate in silence. When I emptied my bowl he took it to the kitchen and when he returned he saw I was half-asleep. He turned the TV off, got me up, and I staggered to the lift, and on up to my room where he tucked me in. I showed a good case of exhaustion.

As usual I was awakened the next morning with the smell of coffee floating up through the vent next to my bed. I got up and dressed in comfortable clothes, and joined Jim in a cup of the brown stuff. I knew the day would be long with three ladies surrounding me as I searched my past. I was no sooner seated in the swing when three cars drove up and three little ladies emerged, waving their hands and telling me to wait for them. They didn't want to miss one single thing.

"Oh, well, I'll start off with little things and build up to more interesting ones," I said after our hugs and hellos. "Jim is on his way out with some coffee for you guys."

Mom was the leader and motivater in our community. She was the first to start many things. She got a petition for the people to sign so at last we would be free of those oil lamps that were forever in use. First Electric (I believe it was First Electric) would come our way, but Mom needed interested people to sign the petition. She couldn't jar those people loose from their old habits and uproot them from their way of life. Mom told them all the advantages they would have with good lighting and many other benefits. She couldn't upseat those hillbillies with a crowbar. I believe she got two signatures which weren't enough. Mom told them that wouldn't stop her from putting electricity in her house. She and Dad discussed their next move. Mom told Dad she was going to town and look around for a Delco generator. This is a motor that would charge a battery that would furnish the electric current for the lights. By the end of the next week we had electric lights in our house. We were the first to have electric lights in our community.

We were also the first to have a motor powered washing machine. I mean with a wringer, boy what a relief that was. It was a Maytag with a small gas motor sitting on the bottom of the machine. We called ourselves advancing with the times.

"Do you gals remember the old washboard?" I asked.

"Annette, what a question. I have rubbed my knuckles raw at times washing my Dads greasy overalls," Bettie said with a disgusted look.

Mom was sick all summer, I believe the year was 1937. I have no idea what was wrong with her. I know Pearl left home that year and went to Memphis, Tennessee, several months before Mom got sick. Dad rose up early each morning and cooked his breakfast and prepared his sack lunch before striking out for his two to three mile walk to work every day. He gave orders for the boys to help me around the house. I can't recall them ever helping me. Every Saturday I washed clothes for five people, sheets and all on the washboard. Dad would tell the boys to keep the washpot boiling for me, but on washday you couldn't find them kids. I was thirteen years old and my hands couldn't reach around Dad's workclothes to wring the things out. I had the clotheslines full each Saturday. Our new Maytag washing machine sure came in handy. When Dad would come in and find out the boys didn't help me, they got their "licking." I probably stretched the point so they could get that extra "lick."

Since Mom was sick all that year I really had my hands full with all of these jobs. Me being the only girl, I had to cook three meals each day. I did all the girl jobs, plus most of the boy jobs. At the time it was no big problem. I was little but I was strong and hard as nails. The doctor told me to feed Mom a lot of chicken broth. I would try to wring a chicken's head off every other day. "Hey girls, I had to stop that job." The last time I tried this, I couldn't get the neck to snap off the body. No matter how hard I tried I couldn't get the neck and the body apart. I wonder why I didn't think about using the ax to finish this job.

Oh well, I dropped the chicken to the ground and it staggered to it's feet and ran a little ways dragging it's head. That scared me. That happened on a Sunday and Dad saw I needed help. He came out of the house and grabbed the chicken off the ground and gave it a quick ring and the hen went scooting a few feet in front of us. I cleaned the thing and when I went to throw the innards out, the darn heart was still beating. I didn't know what was going on with that fowl. I couldn't eat any of that bird.

Mom was so hungry for something sweet. She thought a lemon pie would taste so good. By now Mom was getting up a little each day. She asked Dad if he would make her a lemon pie.

"Katie, tell me what it needs and I'll see what I can do. He made the crust and browned it to a perfect tan and set it aside. Mom told him the ingredients she would need. After she mixed the ingredients, he took the mixture back to the stove to cook until it thickened. He added his lemon juice and filled the cooked crust with the filling. Then he spread the whipped egg whites carefully over the pie and then popped that sucker in the oven until it was golden brown. It was allowed to cool a short time before cutting. Dad then delivered her a slice on one of her prettier plates with fork and napkin. Dad wanted this to be special for her.

Mom sat up in bed, fluffed her pillow, and leaned back ready to tie into the pie she waited so long for. "Oh Jim, it looks so good," she said taking her first bite.

Her eyes lit up and she came out of that bed with one leap spitting and coughing. Dad had taken her a cup and a half of salt rather than sugar when she mixed the filling. He didn't have enough ingredients to make another pie. Poor Mom. Oh, how you can suffer when you are sick. She wanted that pie so bad, but too, she had a good laugh later. By now she was feeling much better and started getting up more.

"Alene, there is more to this 1937 summer. Let me know when you gals need a break."

"We'll let you know," said Alene.

Like I said, Mom was sick all summer. I prepared enough fruits and vegetables to can about one hundred and fifty quarts and pints of vegetables and jams. That summer the government gave us cotton and cloth to make comforters. Miss Tennyson, the county agent, wanted to know if Mom wanted to take this job. Mom always worked close with Miss Tennyson. Mom was the leader of the 4-H club in our community. Since Mom was sick, she couldn't take on this comforter making. I told her I could handle it.

She said, "Frances, you supervise the project and the money is yours."

I jumped at the chance of making a little dough. There was one comforter allowed for each family and they had to shell out a dollar for each one. That summer I made a little cash. The dollar was for me showing these people how to make the comforters. There was no one else in the two communities that wanted to take this job. Mom was really the leader in the two communities. Everybody relied on her.

The year before the comforter making, the government furnished enough cotton and material for each family to make a mattress.

"Were you girls ever in on any of this?"

"No, we never did."

They paid three dollars per mattress. The money was for us, because Mom was the supervisor of this project. She helped them get started with cutting the ticking (the material) and putting in the right amount of cotton. We had scales to weight the cotton on. All of this sewing was done by hand. If anyone wanted our help they forked over an extra dollar. It was sure worth a dollar for the extra help they got. We had a large grove and we had little setups for each family to work under the shade of the trees. Dad would help when he was home. You would put the right amount of cotton in the mattress and sew the end together. Then you would beat it with the broom until it was evenly distributed over the mattress. Then you would sew the roll around the edges. The next step is to tack it at different spots all over the mattress. Everybody needed a new mattress. It was the depression, you know. I still have one of those needles we used that year.

Chapter 11

MY DAYS IN THE COTTON FIELD

"Say, you all grew up with your daddies. Did any of them hide their liquor from your Mom? Mine did. He was so damn sneaky with it. Mom knew when he was drinking," I said, sipping my coffee. "He wasn't an alcoholic but he did drink far to much. We saw how it was ruining some of her brother's lives. And at times it was hurting our family. Lean back and I'll tell you a couple of things that were amusing. What makes it amusing is because he was so sneaky."

As I have said, Dad would move his mill to the woods where they would be harvesting the trees. That is a lot easier on the legs. Some of the hands brought their tents and stayed at the mill camp. It seems that wherever Dad moved the mill he was always in the vicinity of a whisky still. Back in those days a lot of that was going on. Dad could sniff out a bootlegger five miles away. One day we saw Dad coming down the road so tired his butt was dragging. We had a large rose bush, the kind that spread out and covered about a six-foot circle in the front yard. As Dad passed the roses, which were deep red and in full bloom, he tossed his bottle in the backside of this bush. When he got to the front door, he met Mom coming out with scissors in hand to clip a bouquet to grace the center of our round oak table. Dad just shook his head and kept walking on to the house. Of course Mom found his bottle, brought it in and set it on the table. When she wasn't looking, he retrieved his bottle and hid it once more.

Another time when this happened was in Alaska. That state has very long summer days. Mom had a big rhubarb plant at the back of the house. Dad came home from work this particular day and circled around to the back of the house and tossed his bottle in the rhubarb plant. As he walked in the front door he met Mom coming out with a pan and knife in her hand to get enough rhubarb for a pie. Dad kept walking and shaking his head. Mom heard him say, "Damn, she caught me again." Why he hid his liquor has been a family mystery. When Mom died, I was cleaning out her pantry and I found his last bottle with about a third of the whisky left in it. There is no telling how long it had been there. Dad quit drinking several years before he died. I have it in my pantry now. It may turn green with age, but I won't drink it.

"I'll tell you girls three or four quickies before I get out of these hills," I said, taking another sip of coffee.

Johnny and I were home alone one day, doing nothing in particular, so I decided to do a little house cleaning. The first thing I would do is sweep the floor. Johnny has always been pesky. He kept aggravating me. I raised the broom to knock his head off. I missed his head and the force of the broom handle struck his neck full force. That boy went down on the floor. I dropped the broom and ran to his side, thinking that maybe I did some serious damage. Just as I knelt down to check him out, he made a grab for me. I made one leap and I was out of the house in a run. He started chasing me as he rubbed his neck. I told him I was only trying to knock his head off. I didn't mean for the neck to go with it. He finally stopped rubbing his neck and we got so tired running around the house, that we collapsed to the ground and started laughing about the whole event. After awhile he made another dive for me and I started to get out of his way. He just slapped his hands together and started laughing. That was the end of that little spat.

Mom was the Justice of the Peace around 1935 or 1936. It's amazing what people would tell her who wanted her advice. She was good at this job. I think she enjoyed giving advice.

One night around twelve there was a knock on the front door. Mom crawled out of bed to see who was there. At that time of night it had to be important. A young man and his sweetie wanted to get married. Mom married her first and last couple that night. Guess who the witnesses were? Four kids and a dad. We kids really thought that was something. Just think our Mom could marry people. A few years later this couple divorced. I still have Mom's Justice of the Peace seal.

Uncle Edgar was building two rooms on our house. You know kids. They all like to climb. Jimmy and I made our way up the ladder and were perched on one of the rafters deep in conversation about our plans for the future. We were really deep in thought when Johnny sneaked up behind us and squirted our hinnies with his cane squirt gun. It scared us so bad that we liked to have vaulted off the rafter. Of course Johnny did his sidesplitting laugh. When he saw us coming down the ladder, he made himself scarce until our anger ceased.

When Pearl went to Memphis to work that left an odd number at home. A lot of times there were two on one. Didn't matter which two were together, the third one better watch out.

"Did you girls ever smoke or dip?" I asked.

There was no comment. They just looked at me. "Oh well, I'll tell you what Jimmy and I did to Dad's snuff can," I said.

Dad couldn't very well smoke and operate the mill comfortably, so he dipped snuff. Jimmy and I couldn't stand to see any one dip and spit. How sickening! We knew where he would put his snuff can when he came in from work. We caught Dad asleep one evening, so we thought we would teach him a lesson he would never forget. Jimmy got the can of snuff and I went to the kitchen to get the can of red pepper. We put about a fourth teaspoon of the red pepper in the snuff can, put the lid on and gave it a good shake. We then returned the snuff can where we found it.

The next day we saw Dad get his can. Jimmy and I looked

at each other and grinned. When Dad came in that evening, he said nothing. I don't know where he had the other can, but Jimmy and I saw him put his newly purchased can of snuff on the window sill and made marks on each side of the can. We waited for our chance and when we checked it out, we saw two marks on the windowsill. I got the pepper and we doctored it up once again and returned it to the exact spot that was marked. The next day Dad was going to check on a tract of timber and wanted to know if Jimmy and I wanted to go with him. We jumped at the chance for this outing with our dad. We walked behind him going through the woods. After a fashion, he reached into his pocket and pulled out his snuff can. We started getting further and further behind. Dad noticed our actions from the corner of his eye. He never said a word. He tossed the can away and never dipped again. He went to town the next day and bought a weeks supply of chewing tobacco. He told Mom that if those kids hated snuff that bad, he would quit. Well, he still had to spit. Ugh!

You could buy a gallon of milk for a dime and a pound of butter for fifteen cents. When Mom needed milk she would give me a dime and a gallon syrup bucket with a lid for the top. I would wrap a cloth around the wire handle so as not to cut my hands on the mile trip to Mrs. Austin's house and back home. I dropped that dime in the dust one day and it took me thirty minutes before I found it. The dust was an inch or so deep. I was crying.and you can imagine what a mess tears and dust made. I never complained about the work I had to do. I can't recall us complaining about any of our jobs. The boys just didn't want to get the wood in.

"Did you girls ever play in a room full of cotton?" I asked as I saw smiles beginning to form on their faces.

I did say Dad didn't farm. But he must have planted cotton one year, because we had a room full of the soft white fiber. All of us kids would play in the white fluffy stuff. We were in this room one day throwing cotton at one other, when Mom called us in for supper. We were forever racing to the dinner table. I was buried in this stuff. As I got out of the cotton to take my place in the runner's line, I knocked this metal square off the nail it was hanging on. Dad had different things hanging on nails that he would drive in the 2 by 4's. The metal square was at an angle that when it slid off the nail the sharp corner hit me in the center of my head. I saw stars from this blow. I felt to see if I was losing blood. I really thought I detected a little hole there. I began to wonder if I would be meeting my maker right there. I didn't want to die in the cotton, so I staggered in and took my place at the table. I didn't know if I should tell them what happen, or just sit there until I fell out of my chair. And too, maybe this is another one of my battles that I would win. Mom realized something was wrong. I told her what happened. She checked my head and gave me a hug. That made everything better in my book. It seemed like when I played with my siblings, I usually came up on the bloody end of the stick.

Alene said laughing, "So that's your problem."

"Okay, knock it off. Do you want to hear what else I can drag up out of my past? Let's go for a walk first and have lunch. Then we can get down to business," I said waving for Jim to come over. He didn't know I was going to recruit his service for kitchen duty.

"What's up?" he asked.

"We are going for a walk and I know you are just dying to make lunch for us, right?"

"As long as tuna fish is fine with every one," he said waiting for our approval. "That settles it, enjoy your walk."

When we got back, things looked different by my swing. There was this table with a cloth spread over it. A pitcher of cold water and sandwiches were ready for us to dig into. Jim found a vase and stuck a red flower in it. My favorite color. Jim pulled up a chair and joined us. I raised the cloth up to see what was under it. The girls peeked to see what I was looking at.

“Jim, so you’ve made my table I’ve waited so long for, thanks,” I said as I leaned over to give him a hug. “What else have you cooked up for me to do? Better tell me now before I get back to rib stitching,” he said, wiping his mouth with his napkin and heading back to the shop.

“I believe that is all, thanks.”

“Hey gals, I really knew he was working on the table. I went out to the shop yesterday just to stretch my legs a little and he wasn’t there. I had forgotten he was napping. He had just put the last coat of paint on it. How do you like it?”

“Annette, you are lucky to have a handy man around,” Alene said, as Bettie and Della agreed.

We had the first working radio in those hills. It was a Zenith, Mom bought somewhere in the middle thirties. It worked off a hotshot battery. The best that I can remember about this kind of battery is that it was about a foot high and maybe three or four inches thick with a metal casing around it. That was the year boxer Joe Louis won his first, I believe, world title. I know the battery was about dead. Several men in our neighborhood gathered around our radio to see who the next champion would be. They could barely hear it. We kids weren’t allowed to move or even whisper. When Joe won, there were several angry men in our house that night. Everybody expressed their opinion and some weren’t good. I was glad the man won. It was worth it to see such a uproar rising from our house. That was the talk for a long time.

Have you girls spent any time in the cotton fields?” I asked as all three pairs of eyes turned toward me.

“I have,” said Alene. “I got out of the fields by marrying early in life.”

Bettie spoke up, “Was that good or bad, Alene?”

She responded with, “Sometimes I wish I had married later in life like you, Annette. My life would have had a different twist to it. For the better, I hope.”

Dad was sawing for a man about three miles across the woods from our house. This man's adopted daughter was in my class at school. So I went to visit with her one day. Her Dad farmed many acres of cotton. He paid a dollar a day for cotton thinning. That was big money for that moment in time. Walking home that day, I asked my dad if I could work for my friend's Dad in the field. The next day Dad told his boss I wanted to test my skill at thinning the cotton. He told Dad to bring me with him that Monday. I had to get up at three that Monday morning, eat, get dressed, fix my sack lunch, pick up my hoe and file and walk three miles by eight o'clock. The job was already losing its taste. The man was in the field waiting for me. I was the only fair skin gal there. The man appointed this motherly looking woman to be my companion as long as I was in the cotton field. This lady hoed beside me all day. Come noontime we ate our lunch under the same tree. We did everything together for five days. That Friday I got my five dollars, and that ended my cotton chopping days. I have never been so hot and tired in all my life. I told Dad to tell the man I was hanging up my hoe and straw hat and waiting for a better job.

"Della, anyone that wants to know about hoeing cotton, just send them to me. I can give them a little education on this subject without getting out in the fields."

That was the first and last time I hired myself out to thin cotton. Of course, I hoed cotton and corn for Uncle Edgar when he would pull this Tom Sawyer stuff on us. That part was fun. There were other young people with me, and no time limit.

As I have said, we lived in the middle of our community and it was a good stopping off place for people to rest while walking to town. Each summer an aged African-American man would stop by for a drink of water and a little breather before continuing his journey to town. Mom would always offer him something to eat, but I can't recall him ever accepting food. He said his parents were slaves for this certain family that had a large plantation in Mississippi. He was just a kid at the time. He said he sat beside the mistress of the house many times and watched her open up a trunk and count their money. His family was pleased the way they were treated by their owners. He said they were good to them. The man would stop by on his way home for another drink of our cool cistern water. He told Mom the next time he came by, he would bring her the blue speller book that they studied at that time. The next summer when he came by, he brought the speller. Denise has it in her collection of books now. Pearl asked him something about the slave days but he wouldn't answer her.

He said, "Little Missy, I'm not allowed to talk to the little white girls. Tell your mother what you want to know and she will talk to me."

That conversation went on for awhile and then he got up and left. We never saw him again. The man was old. We were sure he had died.

After Pearl left home, I being somewhat of a tomboy, I learned more about fighting, climbing trees and could run as fast or faster than the boys. They had to hustle to beat me in most things. After all, I had to take up for myself. I really had an edge on them, I was Daddy's girl. Remember? One of the twins! Me looking younger than what I was, set me back quite a bit. I wanted to be with kids my own age.

"Hey girls, I'll tell you something else before I leave this area of my young and innocent life," I said propping my feet up in the swing.

I suppose my brothers and I were dreamers. We always had big ideas. We drew up plans for a nine by nine-foot log cabin. We looked for the proper location and decided to build our rugged structure down the hill, by the creek that flowed a little way back of our garden. Bright and early the next day, we took Dad's crosscut saw and the ax and began our task. Johnny and Jimmy would saw the trees down and saw off the length of logs we needed. I would drag the logs to our designated site, notch each end and put them in place. On one occasion I heard, "run Sissy." I look up real fast and saw this little tree coming my way. I dropped what I was doing and left that spot immediately. I thought I'd be crushed. Now the little tree was probably three inches in diameter, but that was enough to get me going. We slaved at this job for days and got the cabin about two feet high, then it started raining. While waiting for the rain to cease, we started naming our route to the cabin with proper names. The creek became known as Possum Creek, the curve was Squirrel Bend, and the hollow became Coon Hollow. We were all set now for our future clubhouse. It eventually stopped raining. When we went to examine our project, we couldn't believe what we saw. Possum Creek had overflowed well over it's banks and floated some of our small logs around in a disarrayed fashion. As we started back up the hill and around Squirrel Bend, we took one last look and said good bye to our little cabin in Coon Hollow. I cannot recall ever going back to rebuild our clubhouse.

During the depression no one had extra money to spend. It was hard for Mom to accept commodities. The state would help people who were in need. It was hard for Mom to accept this kind of charity. In the worst part of the depression, Mom came home with a few commodities and a new outfit for each of us kids. Jimmy got a brown tweed suit. Right off the bat, Johnny and I called him preacher. That infuriated him and he started crying. Johnny got a pair of knickers. The kind that is suppose to be pulled up over the calf of your legs. We started calling him teddy bear and he started crying. I had such a cute dress, they couldn't think of anything to tease me about. Mom dressed Johnny in his new outfit that Monday and told us if we teased him, we would get a whipping when we got home. Now Mom knew better than that. Johnny came home crying and told Mom, "Jimmy called me teddy bear all day at school."

Mom kept her word. She sent Jimmy to get her a peach tree

switch. He notched the thing before he took it to her. When she whacked him with it, the thing broke. She sent Johnny to get her another switch and he brought back a very sturdy one. That Sunday, Jimmy wore his suit to church, and when we got out of sight of Mom, (we walked you know) Johnny started calling him "preacher." That started him crying. Mom would give us some dirty looks at church. She knew what was happening among us kids. Johnny knew his name was mud when we got home. At the house Johnny let Jimmy go in first. Johnny always wanted the last word and too, he knew the jig was up for him. When Jimmy walked passed Johnny, he called him preacher once more. That started the ball rolling. Mom told Johnny to go get her a switch. When he turned to get the little weapon, Mom stopped him and told Jimmy to go get the switch. Of course, Jimmy took Mom a nice sturdy one, hoping Mom would beat the tar out of Johnny. The name-calling went on for a long time, but no more whippings. We just tossed them around and had fun in the process.

"Bettie, did I tell you about our pet goat?" I asked.

"You've told me, Annette, but I bet Della and Alene would like to hear about the poor unfortunate animal."

I have no idea when we got the goat. It made a good pet, but the animal became a pest. Mom looked up the road one morning and saw it following us to school while we were walking across the woods to meet the school bus on another route. She had a rope in her hand and the goat knew what that meant. I can't recall a name for him. Just goat. We had a lot of meatless meals back then. We kept the squirrel and rabbit populations down to a minimum.

Dad had a day off from work one Saturday, so he sat us kids down and we had a long talk. We agreed to let him slaughter the little pest. I watched every bit of this procedure. It must not have bothered us kids because we helped Dad with the cleaning process of this goat, or at least we tried.

That night Mom's slaving over the hot wood stove paid off, or so we thought. She had those delicious biscuits, gravy, vegetables and a platter of steaks. After prayer, the food was passed around and each kid took their steak, except Pearl. Dad took his knife and fork in hand and started cutting a nice juicy bite off the steak. Pearl started bleating like a goat as he was cutting the meat. That stopped all of us. Poor Dad just looked at his steak. He tied into it once again. Pearl let out another goat sound. That did it. Dad pushed his plate back and never touched the steak. Not one of us ate the goat. Pearl didn't know we wouldn't eat the goat. She just didn't want to eat any. The meat was given to Uncle Edgar the next day.

"Girls, this was in the middle of the depression and meat was a royal treat."

With all the hardships the depression brought upon people, Mom held her head high and was a firm believer that she would see us through this. This will also pass. She kept up on the events the ladies were doing in town. Mom didn't miss out on anything. She was available when anyone needed her.

Mom wanted to make a better life for us, while Dad was happy with the way things were. Things have always been like this, why search for a better way? I did not know Dad's inner thoughts. We could have had the finest home on Route Two. Thousands of feet of lumber was out back of our house and we had one of the finest carpenters in our family. Uncle Frank Lawhorn begged Dad to let him build us a house. Labor wouldn't cost a cent. But no, we never got our house. This is the man that raised Dad and his sister Pearl, after their parent's died. Uncle Frank and Aunt Ella moved to West Memphis, Arkansas in the twenties. At one point Uncle Frank had built over half of West Memphis, Arkansas. So we continued living in this small house. Mom always had everything neat and clean. But the house was a little small for the family. Still we managed to have fun.

At that time Jimmy, Johnny and I didn't know we were poor. We had our needs, but not a whole lot of extras. Everyone around us had very little. We had our necessities, and a couple of changes of clothes. That's about all we had. Uncle Edgar never finished building the two rooms he started on our house. We kids were too little before the depression to realize how this would effect our lives. Dad was very prosperous in his line of work. Like I said, at one time we had a nanny. Lots of people lost everything they had. We lost our nanny.

I was grownup enough to know what it was like in the middle of the depression. It seemed like we were always looking for a better way of life. Even though we had good times, we knew we could do better. We did find our escape route when World War II started. All but Johnny started defense work. He was too young at the time.

Mom had her flower garden on one side of our house. She made a table and lawn chairs and painted them white. She arranged them in her flower garden. Her friends knew that when she decided to do something she would go all out. Of course, they admired her table and chairs. She still had her town friends out for tea and great entertainment. She would have these little gatherings when the flowers were in full bloom. We kids knew not to interrupt these precious moments that she cherished so much.

Mom finally sold her land to Uncle Jack. We moved to a larger house with room for the mill on the back of the property. I started working each Saturday at Laser's Variety Store. The hours were from eight a.m. to eight p.m. for $1.50 a day. I don't know how Mom and I got to and from work, but I'm sure it was our four legs doing the job. No wonder I was like a beanpole. I walked everywhere I went.

Chapter 12

My 4-H Club Days

"Ladies, did you know I was a judge in Fayetteville, Arkansas once? I was also a spokesperson in Memphis. Now doesn't that shock you, since I'm no good at neither one. Refill your glasses and I'll tell you how it happened."

In 1938, I went all out with 4-H club stuff. I canned, made my clothes, made curtains for the windows, also covers for the couch. This is when I worked at Lasers on Saturdays.

"Boy, I wish my energy was that strong now. I could have been through with this story yesterday, right?"

The five-year history of my 4-H club days were entered in the Forrest City Times. I won four medals, which I still have. I wasn't the only one sent over to take part in this affair. About twenty of us kids went to Fayetteville, Arkansas in one of our school buses the summer of 1937 or 1938. We stayed in one of the university dormitories. I forget which one. Young people from all over Arkansas were there. By the time we got to our location and in our rooms it started raining. We had two twin beds and three cots in our room. Miss Tennyson, our county agent, came by to take us out for a drive and a sandwich. She put four girls in front with her and six in the back seat. Now that was scary enough. You have a little short women that had nothing but eyeballs level with the steering wheel and it was raining cats and dogs out there, it was time to start praying. I'm serious now. On that little two-lane road I bet she was going every bit of fifty miles per hour. That was fast back then. She found this nice restaurant and as she whipped into the parking lot, she slung girls in every direction. Remember there were no seat belts back then. By now it had stopped raining so we piled out. A couple of older people were sitting in their car watching us unscramble ourselves as we got out of our car. All ten of us girls were taller than Miss Tennyson. The couple next to us just shook their heads in disbelief, backed their car out and drove off. We were all in high school and you know how silly girls can be. We had a ball. I bet Miss Tennyson wished she hadn't taken us with her on this outing. And too, maybe she enjoyed being out with young people.

When we got back to our room, we prepared ourselves for a night of rest. We had to be at our designated areas by eight o'clock the next morning. Some of the girls got in their cots and drifted off to sleep in nothing flat. Dorothy and I had already put our claim on those two beds. We left a light on in the bathroom so we could find our way there if need be. Dorothy punched me and motioned for me to get up. I did. We started with the girls that were in the cots and started turning them over. That got their attention. One girl was trying to get up when Miss Tennyson cracked the door to check on us, then she left. Every one of us had to remake our beds before we went to sleep that night. Dorothy and my beds weren't turned over, but they were stripped and we had to make them up before we could retire.

I was in the baking department and my job was to judge cakes. You may consider that an easy job. But a few beads of sweat popped out on me. One of the girls modeled a dress and won second prize. You can see sad as well as happy faces at these events. A teenager in front of me fell as we were heading for the cafeteria. He was on crutches and I noticed he didn't bend his knees. He fell flat and I didn't know what to do. By the time Dorothy, Doris and I and others gathered around him, he was up.

I was the only person that went with Miss Tennyson to the Tri-State Fair in Memphis, Tennessee that same year. One of the young teenage boys had made bedroom furniture for his 4-H project and I had to explain his workmanship. I don't know why he didn't tell about his own project. Maybe he did and this was just a break for him. I know he left when I took over. People did come by and were forever asking questions about this handsome bed and chest of drawers. When the young man got back, he took over. Miss Tennyson and I had lunch in Memphis, then we headed back to Forrest City. This wasn't near as much fun as the Fayetteville trip.

"Did you ladies ever chew gum in school? I did in one class. It happened like this."

Since I was first in alphabetical order, I occupied the first seat in the first row in English class. Miss Martin was a single teacher who didn't seem to like me. I don't know what caused the distance between us. Clarence sat behind me. Thelma was across from me and behind her was Bobby.

Everyday Clarence would bring gum to school from their store. It was always in Miss Martin's class that he wanted to share his gum. I would feel a finger poke me in my back and I knew what to do. He would put two sticks of gum in the side of his shoe and slide his foot down to the side of my desk. I would reach down and get the gum. I would put one stick in the side of my shoe and shuffle my foot close enough for Thelma to extract the gum with one quick motion. In the meantime Clarence was doing the same for Bobby. We four would set there and chew our gum when Miss Martin wasn't looking in our direction, or so we thought. I don't know why she would catch me chewing and not the other three. She would ask, "Frances, are you chewing gum?" I would say, "yesum." I got where I would swallow the stuff and say, "No ma'am." She knew I was but she couldn't see it.

We were in the sixth grade. Clarence, Bobby and Thelma were never caught and they didn't swallow their gum. Clarence continued to bring gum and we would go through this ritual every day and Miss Martin would ask, "Frances, are you chewing gum?" One day as we were going to another class, I told my three friends that if I was brave enough I would offer her a stick of our gum. I wonder if she would have taken it? I'll never know.

"Alene, I can not believe you girls were all that nicy, nice in school. Oh well, maybe Arkansas was a better play ground for innocent mischief." You know girls will always keep their eyes cocked on cute boys. I was no different. I was so bashful when it came to boys, it hurt. There would be three classes in study hall. This is in high school now. Bobby sat in front of me in study hall and we would talk every chance we got. I had something brilliant to say one day so I gave him a sneaky tap on the back and he spun around to hear what I had to say. I whispered something to him and when I looked up I saw Mrs. Halbrook looking at me. She motioned for me and I approached her. I knew she had something distasteful in mind. She told me to write "I must remember to remember not to talk without permission" one hundred times. I learned to write with two pencils pretty good. When I returned to my seat Bobby twirled around and asked me what did she want. Before I said anything I looked to see if the teacher was looking. She was. She motioned for me to tell Bobby she wanted to see him. On his way back to his seat he stuck up one finger and then made two O's with his fingers. I knew he had the same assignment I did.

"Remember girls, that I worked all day each Saturday for only $1.50." I would buy my lunch for fifteen cents a day. That got me a nickel coke and a ten-cent hamburger. I saved seventy-five cents each week. I started a little savings account. Jimmy was working on Saturdays at the bakery, but somehow I managed to save more than he did.

We had a history school trip coming up the summer of 1939. It would cost $25.00. Our destination was Washington, DC. We were told about the trip several months in advance. That would give the kids time to save up enough money for the trip. Jimmy nor I had enough for both of us to go. We made a pact between ourselves. Whoever had the most money saved by trip time the other one had to forfeit their savings. I managed to save fifteen dollars and Jimmy had ten. He handed it over without one whimper. It was a little sad because I knew he wanted to make the trip with us. But I took the money and ran. We gave the teacher fifteen dollars and each person kept ten. Boy, money went a long way back then. The fifteen dollars paid for our lodging for a week or more, two special dinners and to attend one show, I believe at the Ford Theater, or was it another one? We bought all but two of our meals and any presents we wanted to take back home with the ten bucks.

We went to the White House, the Capital and the Smithsonian. We saw George Washington's Mount Vernon, Arlington National Cemetery, the tomb of the Unknown Soldier, the History and Technology Museum, and the Federal Security Building. The lift took us up 555 feet to the top of the Washington Monument. We saw a lot of the Civil War relics in the museums all through the Carolinas, Virginia and Tennessee. Would you believe I got back home with a $2.00 bill and some change. I handed out three gifts that I bought with great pride. I brought the $2.00 bill back because I thought it was bogus. I kept that bill in my purse for years.

While I was singing in the church choir in 1948 in Anchorage, Alaska a service man went through my purse and stole all my money including five two dollar bills. This was a great trip back in those days. I wish Jimmy could have made the trip with us. To his day I still owe him ten dollars. That's okay. When I married and left Alaska, Jimmy owed me much more than that so let's call it even.

Chapter **13**

World War II and Entering Defense Work

"Do you girls know where you were and what you were doing when World War II started on December 7, 1941?"

Many of our seniors were signing up for service. Some of the teachers brought their radios to school so we could keep current with the news. I think everyone bowed their heads when we learned that one of the boys from Forrest City High was among some of the first to be killed overseas. Everything became distant and different. Many teachers quit their jobs and joined the defense work to help defend our country. People went in all directions. I went to Fisher Aircraft in Memphis.

This was a good time for me to leave the nest, shake the dust out my hair and look for a brighter side of life. At least money wise. I approached Mom with the idea of me quitting school and starting defense work. I told her I could make seventy-four cents an hour at Fisher Aircraft. That beat $1.50 a day at Lasers. I'm sure he paid more later, but I didn't want to stick around and find out. My chest was already bulging with pride. I gave Mom my solemn promised that I'd finish my senior year in a private school in Memphis. I did graduate from Mitchell's Private School May 17, 1944. Graduation was held at the Hotel Peabody in the Louie the 5th room, I believe.

I moved in with Pearl and her husband, Lynn Willis, in Memphis. I signed up to work at Fishers, February 1942. I picked up my first rivet gun and started my two weeks of training. I met my twin girl friends, Lurline and Pauline Coleman, there and we were friends long after I left Fisher's. At Fisher Aircraft, we built the B-25, the Billy Mitchell Bombers.

My first job was on the bomb-bay doors as a "bucker". A bucker is the person that holds a piece of iron behind the rivet to flatten it as the riveter pounds it on the other side of whatever you are riveting. This riveting job holds the two pieces of metal together. Not long after the bomb-bay door job, I was moved to another department. At first this long table looked scary. It had a half moon hole at one end of the table with a ridiculous looking apparatus extended in the half circle. It looked like big long jaws reaching out to grab you. It was called a "dimpler". I dimpled the holes in the wings so countersunk rivets could be used. This made the outside skin completely smooth. I learned to make this dimpler sing. You could hear me working all over the department.

I got pretty fast dimpling each hole and never making a mistake until this government inspector decided to stop by every day to watch me in action. When I knew he was watching me, I would get nervous and miss the hole and dimple the skin, which meant a patch had to be put on to cover the hole. I don't know why the man made me nervous, but too, I was extremely self-conscious. He started watching me work at a distance and when I had finished what I was working on he would come over and we would talk. He was a little flirty, which I kinda liked.

"You know girls, if I had paid more attention to him I could have had me a little Government Inspector feller," I said rearranging myself in my seat. "The next thing I must do is get a long cushion for this swing. It gets pretty hard before the days end," I commented.

I rode to work with my boss, Richard Byrd. Three other people would accompany Richard and me in his two seater A-Model Ford. We had more fun in this car. You could actually hear the car putt-putting two blocks away. I think he had the oldest car on this large Fisher parking lot. We all lived a short distance from each other. We worked on the swing shift, which was from four till twelve o'clock midnight.

A young man by the name of Don rode with us. He was some good-looking guy. Don was telling us one evening that he had a skating date and she stood him up. Don looked at me and asked me if I wanted to go skating. I looked at Don as I kidded him and said, "Don, I'll have to ask my mamma." I thought Richard was going to wreck his little Ford right there. I would have gone with him if he hadn't asked me in front of the others. I thought, man what have I done. I lost out here. I really wanted to go with him. He never asked me for another date.

I think changing my location at that point was the best thing I could have done. You can stay in one place for so many years that it doesn't give your mind enough room to expand. I felt proud that this new growth was taking place within me. I'm glad I left the hills of Arkansas and found room for expansion.

"Della, have you girls ever eaten at the Hotel Peabody dinning room?" I asked. I saw three no, head shakes.

I got a group of Fisher girls together one day for a dinner out. Some of these girls were a little hesitant. It sounded like some of them hadn't completely cut themselves loose from their mother's apron strings. Eight girls showed up at the assigned door at the Peabody. It's strange how those girls stood back for me to enter the building first and on to the dining room. Of course Lurline and Pauline were behind me. We were escorted to this round table in front of the stage. We had the white tablecloth, napkins and the works. The waiter brought our water and gave us our menus and left. They asked me what was I ordering. I told them chicken gizzards. I have no idea why I chose gizzards. I gave my gizzard and milk order first. Would you believe everyone except Lurline and Pauline chose those silly gizzards. I put my napkin on my lap. Just like clockwork they did the same. Lurline and Pauline were noticing the girls doing what I did. They were setting there with smirks on their faces. Mom taught me and my siblings table manners and the proper way to set the table as soon as we were old enough to understand this. It does pay off somewhere down the line.

Pauline and I got our heads together and decided on coconut pie for dessert. Everybody chose the same. I got a piece of paper from my purse and jotted down my favorite song and handed it to the waiter. He took it to the stage and handed it to the bandleader. They played my song. Those girls sat there with their mouths opened, so to speak. They couldn't believe what I had done. I told them I saw others do it so why can't they play our song.

It may be a little odd, but I wasn't all that timid around girls. I could get things started and see it through. As for the boys, if they were good talkers I could join in and I wasn't so nervous. I just couldn't start the conversation very good.

After awhile the waiter brought our tickets and I put a quarter tip by my plate. Hey, you girls are laughing but each person placed their quarter by their plate which was pretty good back in those days. Everybody enjoyed there dinner. The same group of girls never went out together again. It did look like four of the girls had never been in a place that nice before. Three of the girls did join the skating parties I organized once a week for the remainder of my stay at Fisher Aircraft.

My family chose to be tackers and welders at Ingalls Shipyard in Pascagoula, Mississippi. I don't know why Mom didn't enter Johnny in school there. Maybe he and our cousin didn't get along. Aunt Virgie and her daughter, Jerrie, went to Pascagoula with Mom and Dad and shared the same apartment. That puts two kids together that weren't compatible. So I ended up with Johnny. He played hooky most every day. The truant officer was calling me every week. But we did have fun.

Before I sent him back to Mom, I took him on one of our skating parties. This is the first time Johnny was ever on roller skates so far as I know. He put those skates on and made his way to the middle of the rink and all he could do was go. He had nothing to hold on to. He knew he could master the skates. That boy got started and couldn't stop. He didn't fall either. Lurline, Pauline and I laughed so hard we had to sit down. His mouth was wide open with arms and legs floundering in all directions. He looked like a scared ape going down an oil slick hill. I have never seen anything so wild looking. After six laps around the rink he figured he had to stop, so he ran into the wall. He crawled over to me as I sat on the bleacher laughing hysterically at how foolish he looked.

He said, "Sissy, would you help me get these damn things off?"

I thought the best thing to do was to send him back to Mom. I couldn't handle him. I just couldn't keep the kid in school. He became friend's with a paperboy and he would ride the bike with him and throw his papers. I never knew where he would go when I went to work. So I tossed him back to Mom.

Johnny went to Mitchell's Private School for awhile. I don't know why he quit Mitchell's. But he checked in at a regular school. From that time on I couldn't keep up with the kid. He was forever playing hooky. I thought this kid don't belong to me so Mom got her number two son back. He needed better control than what I could do.

Chapter **14**

My First Train Ride

When I was in the country, I thought man, it's a big world out there. I told Mom when I left those hills that I never intended to come back there to live. Some of the most miserable years of my life were spent on Route Two as well as some of the happiest ones. Richard Byrd was a good boss. When I would catch up on my "dimpling" job I would help other girls on their jobs. So I worked on wing tips, nose cones, and other jigs that I long forgot what they were called. I would help get the burrs off the drilled holes before they were dimpled. I kept pretty busy. I made top salary pretty fast. I went from 74 to 89 cents per hour all within a year. You could never get more than a nickel raise at a time. Richard saw all that I did, so he put me in for another raise. He told me not to tell anyone else there because 89 cents was the tops in what we were doing. There was a smile on his face when he handed me my check that Friday. I knew I had my raise so I looked him square in the eye and winked, and thanked him. I was raised to 94 cents an hour. That was big money back then. In spite of my shyness I was still a little flirt at 19.

Brother Jimmy worked at Ingalls as a machinist. Just before he reached the age of eighteen, he joined the Navy. He didn't want to be drafted into the Army. He took his training in Virginia. It came time when he would be shipped out to sea. He told Mom when he would be home on leave before being shipped out. Mom called me and then I called Pearl in Forrest City. We made arrangements to go to Pascagoula to see our little brother before the wind hit his sails.

I told Richard a month in advance that I wanted a leave of

absence. He told me not to worry, that he'd see that I got my leave. For three weeks he'd tell me it would be no problem. The last week I asked every day if I had my leave. He kept putting me off. That Friday I asked him if he had my leave. He told me he didn't get it and I couldn't go. I told him I was going to see Jimmy and I didn't care what he said. He could turn me in to the head boss if he wanted to because I was going. I had the shipyard on my mind, and too, I didn't want to be fired from Fishers for not getting a leave. When I left my department that Friday I looked at Richard and told him bye, I'd see him when I got back. I never thought that would be the end of our friendship.

I met Pearl at the train station that Saturday for the long ride to Pascagoula. I had my hair so pretty with my wavy bangs. It was snowing pretty hard that day. I passed a window as I entered the train station and I saw my reflection. I thought how pretty I looked with so much snow in my curls. When we went to the restroom I took another look at my beautiful hair and all I saw was a straight, unruly mess. I wanted to cry. Pearl said, "Here, let me fix it." When she got through combing my hair, it was still a mess. When it gets wet the stuff straightens out. We were to stay two weeks in Pascagoula. While there, I saw how much fun my family was having on the coast. I started thinking about my move one day to this coastal town.

When I returned to work I had a red tag on my time card telling me to come to a certain office. This middle-aged man asked me why I didn't get a leave of absence. I told him that my boss knew about this a month ahead of time. The last week I would ask him every day if he had my leave. That Friday he said I couldn't go. This fellow asked me who was my boss. I told him Richard Byrd. He told me the next time I wanted a leave to come see him. I thanked him and he punched a little button and I walked out the door. When I got back to my department Richard had already been transferred to who knows where. I never did find out where he was. Although I did see him from time to time in different places in the plant. I hated to see him removed from our department, because I liked Richard. He was a good boss. To this day I don't know why he didn't get me the leave he promised me. I had moved long before this happened and no longer rode to work with him.

I had moved into a small kitchenette (a kitchenette is one room with bed, cook stove and icebox in the same room) in the same house my friends, Lurline and Pauline, were in. After about three months in this dwelling, our landlady was going to raise our rent from $5.00 a week to $10.00. We knew she couldn't do that because due to the war the rent was frozen. She informed us that she was going to throw our clothes out into the yard if we didn't pay her the increase in rent. Lurline and I found out whom we should see about our odd situation. We were all set that Saturday to see the proper authorities. Pauline was to stay in her room and listen to the phone conversation, if there would be any. The hall phone was by their bedroom door.

Lurline and I went downtown to this certain building and got into the elevator that would take us up to the 27th floor in one straight shot. I thought my head was lodged in my chest that trip was so fast. We could hardly walk because our legs were so weak. We entered the office and told this good-looking guy what our landlady was going to do to us.

He said, "She can't do that, she should know rent is frozen until after the war." He asked for her phone number, which we gave him. Now that is why Pauline stayed back home. She heard every word of that end of the conversation. When thc parlay was over, our landlady slammed the receiver down very hard and went to her room in a huff. This gentleman said if she gave us anymore trouble to let him know. From then on our landlady had very little to do with us, but she didn't hesitate in collecting her five bucks for each room. We were three, very determined twenty-year-old girls and we knew our rights even though we were fresh from the country.

"Have you girls ever been shot at?" I asked.

"Of course we haven't," Bettie said with a puzzled look on her face. "Why, were you?"

I wasn't shot at, I was just standing in the line of fire. I wanted to go uptown. Lurline and Pauline didn't want to go with me, so I went alone. I walked the three blocks to the bus stop. You usually always had to wait for the bus. I was standing in the shade of this big oak tree at the bus stop when bullets came my way, clipping leaves from the tree I was standing under. As two or three leaves landed on my head another shot rang out. One shot hit a young boy riding on his bike, while his buddy passed by like a rocket. Another shot passed me and went through the window of the house on the corner where I was standing. The lady was lying on her bed and she raised up her window and wanted to know what was going on. I told her I didn't know what the excitement was all about. The boy that was hit fell off his bike and crawled to the curb while the other boy kept pedaling. By that time a man went over to see where the boy was hit. I followed a few people over to where the man was attending this young boy. This gentleman saw blood coming out of the toe of the boy's shoe. He immediately started taking the shoe off. The bullet took the boy's little toe off. In a few minutes a police car drove up with a woman in the back seat crying.

These boys had delivered her a telegram a week before that said her son was killed in action. It pushed her over the edge. She wanted to kill these two boys that delivered the sad telegram. She waited each day for them to pass her house. She sat on her front porch with a loaded rifle until they finally showed up. When she saw them pedaling by her house she raised her rifle, aimed it very recklessly and started firing away as fast as she could reload it. The lady with the rifle could have gotten me as I waited for the bus, also the lady that was lying on her bed in her bedroom. I do believe in divine protection because I've had too many narrow escapes. Come to think of it, it was a good thing that my friends didn't go with me that day. One of us could have stopped one of those bullets. Lurline and I were closer buddies and we usually went places together. But that day I stood alone under that oak tree. Would you believe with bullets coming my way, it didn't scare me.

Chapter **15**

I Quit Fisher Aircraft and Move To Pascagoula, Mississippi

"Let me tell you girls a funny thing that happened on the street car once when I lived in Memphis," I said as I rearranged myself in my seat.

Many people rode the public transportation at that time. There would be crowds of people standing in the aisles and hanging onto a metal bar that extended from the ceiling. One crisp winter day the streetcar was stuffed with people. An older gentleman dressed up in his office suit noticed his fly was unzipped. So he reached down to zip it up hoping no one would notice him. There was a lady jammed up next to him wearing a fur coat. Somehow he got some of the fur caught in the zipper and couldn't get it out. The lady noticed what had happened so she started assisting him in his efforts. People realized what was going on around them and started watching this procedure. Everybody began laughing at this bizarre situation. When it came time for her to get off the streetcar, he had to go with her. Have you ever seen a man blush? A man did that day. As far as the people could see them, they were still trying to get the fur out of the zipper without too much damage to the fur.

"Are you girls getting tired of me chattering? Alene, it is pretty warm here even under the shade tree. Do you want to run and get us something cool?" I asked as Bettie, Della and I got up to unwind and limber up a bit. Alene is seven years younger than we are so we let her do the legwork. Sometimes she surprises us with what she brings out.

"Now, don't lose your train of thought," said Alene as she

started toward the house.

She returned and handed each of us a frosty beer. How refreshing. We should have thought of this earlier. Right? I became a friend with a girl that worked at the aircraft plant by the name of Mary. Her ex-husband lived in Pascagoula and they thought about getting back together. So that started me thinking about my next move. I hated to leave Lurline and Pauline. They were two of my dearest friends, but family blood was calling. My friends weren't too far from Coldwater, Mississippi, their hometown, and I was a long way from my folks. After a year and four months at Fisher, Mary and I went to the office and checked out. As we walked out the side door, we really did have tears flowing. We looked back for one last time and saw our matron friend standing in the doorway. We gave her one last wave. That was the last time I saw her. While visiting my aunt in Memphis a year later, I went by to see Lurline. Pauline had married and moved to some other part of Memphis. That was the last time I saw any of the girls I ran with in Memphis.

Mary and I rode the train to Pascagoula. Her ex and my family were waiting for us with open arms. This started a new chapter in my life.

When you would quit one defense job there was a waiting period before you could start another one. I long forgot why this waiting was necessary. After a week in Pascagoula my insurance agent came to collect my dues. They did that back then, today you mail them in. He told me he could get me signed up at the shipyard with no waiting period, because he had a friend that worked in the employment office that owed him a favor. He told me who to ask for and to be on the outside of the employment office at eight o'clock the next day. He said that when he came out of the office he would just look at me and nod his head. I was to go in and ask to speak to a certain person. Everything went as planned. When I entered the office there was a short line of people on one side. I saw a man standing behind the counter further down on the other end of the counter fiddling with some papers. He looked up as I walked toward him. I introduced myself and asked for this certain person. He said, "That's me." He took me to his desk and I was signed up for a two week training course as a tacker for the shipyard starting that Monday. What a great contrast between Fisher Aircraft and Ingalls Shipyard. At Fisher Aircraft the planes were made out of aluminum alloy, the ships out of iron, I guess it was pure iron. I loved them both.

Brother Jimmy was already in the Navy somewhere in the middle of the Pacific Ocean. Johnny and I started working at the shipyard about the same time. He a welder and myself a tacker. We became close buddies in spite of our age differences. I was twenty but looked as young as Johnny. We did everything together. We had a group of young people we ran with. Before Jimmy left for the Navy, he and Mom got a Presbyterian Church started in our area. The minister from town came out each Sunday to deliver the sermons. Later funds were raised to build a church in our neighborhood.

There were from ten to fifteen of us young people that banded together each weekend. We enjoyed our beach parties and midnight wiener roast on the sandy beaches of the Gulf of Mexico. We had something going every weekend. Billy, our soda jerk friend, worked at one of the drugstores that had the best soda fountain in town. It had several stools at the bar. We would try to sit two to a stool. Each one of us came from the country and had no fat on our bones. Country kids usually worked in the fields and they sure did walk a lot before the war. That kept our weight down. If we worked it right two could fit on a stool with some comfort but in an odd fashion.

Billy knew what we wanted and knew we would make it rough on him because we would order different flavors of malts and sodas each time. Ten to fifteen of these drinks kept the old boy busy. Billy would make thick ones with chunks of strawberries and pieces of pineapple that would stick to the end of our straws as we would try to suck up the delicious malted flavor. Back then everything was made with real ice cream. After his workday ended he would join us in our youthful frolicking.

After my two weeks of training I was ready to start putting a ship together. I was put on the first ship to work in the cabins. My shipfitter gave me a job where I had to stand on a bench and reach up to fill a little hole in the side of one of the partitions. Can you imagine me using enough of this welding stuff to fill a little hole! I was brand new with this tacking. That hole was getting bigger and bigger. This was a hot day and sweat was pouring off of me. Every time I touched my rod to the medal the thing would stick. I was nervous to start with. They could have given me a job that was on my level. That next week I was transferred to another ship four "ways" over. A "way" is what the space is called when building a ship from the keel up to the cabins. It is the space the ship occupies before launching. There were ten "ways" in dry dock and at least ten in wet dock. There was a ship launched at least once a week, or it sure seemed like it. When the dry dock crew finished their job, the ships were launched and taken to the wet dock and put in place by the tugboats. The wet dock crew would continue the finishing touches and make ready for use. I don't really know but these ships were, probably, cargo ships.

I would work with a muscular short-legged shipfitter by the name of James Ward and Carl, a small scrawny guy that served as our "burner." My first job with my new crew took me three decks down. Ward said he would pull my welding line down for me. I would take my welding rods and follow. Before I left the main deck, Bob our ship boss, approached me and told me I was to pull my own line from now on. I said okay and started climbing down to the third deck.

Ward and our area boss, Scarbrough, saw Bob talking to me and wanted to know what he said. "Ward, he told me to pull my own line from now on," I said as I took a seat on the cold metal. I learned what boss was on our ship by the stripe on their hard hat. One stripe was the smallest boss, and on up to three or more. Scarbrough had one stripe.

Ward and Scarbrough left Carl and me for a lengthy time. When Ward returned he told us what happened. He said Bob had no right telling me what he did and he would pull my welding line anytime he wanted to. Ward and Scarbrough didn't like Bob and they were gathering enough information to get him removed from our ship, and what he said to me did it.

I had an OK badge, which meant I could work anywhere on the ship. I had no idea where that badge would take me. A shipfitter needed a tacker to tack a lug on the side of the hull so he asked Ward if he could borrow me for the job. Ward told me to go weld the lug on for him. I put my helmet on my head and hooked my bag full of welding rods on my belt and followed this tobacco spitting man to the edge of the ship. I had no idea I had to go down this "upright." An "upright" is an iron square that had rungs on all four sides like a ladder that you went up and down on if necessary. It also was used to support the scaffolds that went around the ship from the bottom to the top of the ship at different intervals. Now I was on the top deck and I'm deathly afraid of heights. As long as I have something to support me I'm all right. But me hanging there in open space, it liked to have got to me. I really shook when I stepped out on the first rung of the upright. Nothing but scrap iron in a tangle mess a hundred feet or so below me. I felt like I was going to turn loose any minute. I almost froze to the upright and I had to go down to the second scaffold.

There were two large pieces of iron that didn't fit right. One sunk in about an eighth of an inch. I was to tack a "lug" on the low side. A "lug" is a square piece of iron with a hole in the middle. A fishtail jack could be used to pull the two pieces together that were to be welded. I was going to make fast work out of this so I pulled my hood down and started this job in haste. After a few seconds the guy touched me on the shoulder and I stopped. He wanted to see if the lug was in the right spot. He lifted the jack up and fitted it into the hole. This whole procedure was about waist high for me. He told me to go ahead and finish the weld and he would hold the jack in place. I started back welding. Suddenly I felt something hit in front of me and violently shake the scaffold. The shipfitter grabbed me. I raised my hood to see what happened. The jack was about three feet long and weighed a good thirty pounds. Instead of knocking me off the scaffold, somehow the jack jumped forward and landed in front of me. By now I had a good spell of the shakes. I pulled my hood down and made a swat at the welding job. I pushed my hood up when I finished and I didn't stop until I hit the main deck. I went straight to Ward and told him what happened.

Ward was waiting for this shipfitter when he arrived after finishing his job on the side of the ship. I don't know what Ward was saying to him, but you can use your own imagination. He could spit out a few choice words when he felt like it, but never around me. He wouldn't allow anyone to curse or tell off-color jokes in my presence, either. I must say that I have worked with some pretty nice folks in my life. He never loaned me out again.

"Girls, I'll tell you something else that could have taken my life instantly. It is strange how I didn't fear anything at age twenty. I was fearless except for heights. Now as long as I'm in an enclosure with heights, I'm okay."

One day four of us was standing by the cabins waiting for the twelve o'clock whistle. Ward and Carl were standing in front of Scarbrough and me. Just goofing until the whistle blew for lunch. There was a burner on top of the cabins burning bolts off of two pieces of iron, which was pretty dangerous. When each bolt released the pressure off the two large pieces of iron, they would go flying off in different directions. For no reason at all I went and stood by Ward. The instant that I moved, one of those big bolts hit in the exact spot I had moved from. Ward saw what happened and he grabbed my hard hat and slapped it on my head and said, "Kid, never take that hat off your head as long as you are on this ship." He always called me Kid. If the bolt had come down on my head it would probably have gone half way through me before it stopped. It was a piece of iron coming down from the sky.

Most everyone brought their lunch and at noon people were scattered all over the shipyard to consume their meal and rest for an hour. My girlfriend and I enjoyed heading for the scaffold just above the water and feeling the cool breeze blowing as we stretched our tired bodies out on the wide planks while we ate our lunch, and watched those beautiful dolphins at play. I did not have to go down an upright to get to this scaffold. It was the bottom one that protruded out over the water.

You know, the seagulls were very friendly at lunchtime. One day I was standing at the foot of the gangplank, about to make my way back up when I saw Ward just ahead of me. On the platform at the top of the gangplank Scarbrough was shining a red apple and holding it up for Ward to see before he started eating it. He gave it another shine on his shirt and held it up for another look. Ward was just about ready to take it away from him when Scarbrough gave it one more shine. He held it up once again and a seagull dove down and took the apple out of his hand. "Girls, that was funny looking. Just seeing Scarbrough dancing around in front of a hungry seagull. I thought Ward would tumble down the gangplank he laughed so hard."

"Della, you like to dance and do the high kick, right? I'll tell you something Dad did back in 1942 while heading for his welding job in wet dock." There was a wide roadway leading to the main gate of the shipyard. On both sides of this long walkway were several beer joints with their doors flung open and music flowing out of each establishment. Aunt Virgie and Dad were walking past one of these joints heading for work.

They came by one bar that reeked with the smell of beer and vibrating with loud music. Dad stopped, handed Aunt Virgie his lunch bucket and started doing his buck dance without saying one word. People stopped to watch this lively performance. When the music ended he took his lunch bucket from Aunt Virgie and walked on and never cracked a smile. Everybody laughed and gave him a big hand. Aunt Virgie just threw her head back and laughed all the way to her ship.

We lived in a rented apartment in the maritime housing that was apparently navy built. It had two to three apartments all hooked together in one string. We had a three-bedroom apartment on the north end of one of these strings. It was one of our goof-off Sundays for Dad, Johnny and me. We were doing nothing. I don't know what Johnny said to irritate Dad to the point where he wanted to tie into that boy. Dad jumped up off the couch and started for his number two son with a vengeance. Johnny stood up and looked Dad right in the eyes and said, "Dad, while you are getting yourself a meal, I'll get me a sandwich." In other words, Johnny wasn't about to stand there and let Dad whap him one. The whipping days for all of us were over long ago. Dad backed off laughing.

As I have said there were several of us young people that ran together. We were forever linking our arms together and stretching out across the road. One night coming from church we assembled ourselves in this fashion. As we would pass each of our houses, that person would fall out and head for their house and the rest of us would keep going. This particular night I was on one end and Ernest was on the other. Not one of us girls would date him but he was in our group. We came by his residence and he uncoupled his arm and headed for his house. All of a sudden we heard someone running up behind me. He kissed me on the check, and turned around and went on his way. It was a dark night. Those girls strained their eyes to look at me and ask, "Was that Ernest?" I said, "Yes it was and it better not go any further." No, the kidding didn't stop.

I missed sister Pearl. While in Memphis I could go to Forrest City, Arkansas for the weekend to see her any time I wanted to. In Pascagoula, we were worlds apart. This might have been a dirty trick but after work one Friday I approached my Dad and said, "Dad, we are going to see Pearl, you want to make the trip with us?" He said, "You better tell Katie to get ready. No point getting there at midnight." Then I would high tail it to Mom and tell her that Dad said if she was going with us to see Pearl she better get her hinny in high gear. Those tactics worked every time. I was always the first to shower and pack my over night bag because I knew what was going on.

Chapter 16

Some of Pearl's Stories

"Do you girls want to hear some of Pearl's boners she pulled when she lived in Palestine?" I asked as I rearranged myself in the swing. "I've got to make a thicker cushion for this thing."

"Yes, but let me go inside first," said Alene as she got up to make a fast trip to the house.

"Alene, stop by the kitchen and bring a pitcher of ice water. This has all vanished," yelled Bettie.

Alene hollered out the kitchen window and asked, "How about this cold bottle of wine?"

Bettie answered, "Sounds okay to me, bring it on."

I have been making wine for a number of years now. I can make it as good, if not better, than some of the wineries. Volume may have something to do with it. I make mine two gallons at a time. The little ladies always look forward to hitting my wine rack to see what I have new on the shelf.

"Are you girls getting tired of me rambling on. I get on a roll and it's hard to stop," I said getting up to stretch a bit.

Lynn, Pearl's husband, was a lot older than she was. He managed to get her anything she wanted within reason. He built her many houses, each one she designed a little different until she arrived at what she wanted. Lynn bought several acres of land in Palestine, Arkansas. He thought he would try his hand at growing rice. He did that for one year. Pearl thought she would get in the chicken business and sell eggs. She got tired of that and Lynn sold the chickens and bought her a few cows. She thought she was going to get rich selling milk. Why she wanted to try her hand at chickens and cows is beyond me. That was not like my sister back home in the country. She got an African-American lady by the name of Mary to help her with all of her everyday chores. Pearl got tired milking so she sold her cows.

Pearl kept this lady employed to help with her next adventure. She enjoyed help around her country home two and three times a week.

One day a traveling salesman came by pulling a small trailer that was full of groceries, behind his car. He stopped by Pearl's house, hoping to make a great sale. He told her he was getting pretty tired of being away from home so much. Pearl thought she would relieve him of this burden and asked him if he wanted to sell the store. They agreed on a price. Pearl bought the whole store, trailer and all. He backed the trailer up to an appropriate location in her large yard, took his money and left. Before Mary went home that day she went to the store and bought several dollars worth of groceries. She put her groceries on the porch and followed Pearl into the house. Pearl went to the bedroom and Mary followed her. About that time Lynn came in. Pearl went to her pillow, pulled her pistol out and pointed it toward Lynn and said. "Lynn, I know what you have been doing and I'm tired of it." Mary jumped between them and was begging her not to shoot Mr. Lynn, because he hadn't done her any wrong. Lynn knew what Pearl was doing and he played along with her. They argued and threatened each other for awhile and poor Mary was near to tears. After a fashion Mary realized they were kidding around again.

When Lynn left the room Mary started to sit on the cedar chest. Pearl yelled, "Mary, don't sit on my dead husband's coffin." That scared the fire out of Mary. She told Pearl she didn't want the groceries because they may be haunted. She started out the back door on a run. Pearl caught up with Mary and told her that wasn't a coffin, it was her cedar chest.

"Mary, the place isn't haunted," Pearl said. Pearl didn't

want to lose a sale.

Mary stopped right there and started this hysterical laughter and said, “Miss Pearl, I finally got one on you.” She went back and got her groceries and laughed all the way home. Pearl just watched her in awe, and wondered how her prank turned on her so fast.

James Polk Alderson and Kathryn Orene Smith in 1918,
a year before their marriage.
Dad always cocked his hat to one side
....never knew why.

Annette, Pearl and Frankie Alderson.
Our first portrait together.

Johnny and Jimmy Alderson
The little men of the house

Me and my twin girl friends when we worked at Fisher Aircraft. We were three monkeys in monkey suits.

Me on the end with some of my friends when I worked at Ingalls Shipyard. We threw in a couple of sailors to impress our friends back home.

Pascagoula pier and the fun we had swimming in the Gulf of Mexico

Drinking in a cool stream

The Alderson's one year before
we went to Alaska in 1947

Our campsite at Sweetgrass, Montana

July 1948
Waiting for the Canadians to get through with their official celebration of the opening of the Alcan Highway, before we could continue our trip to Alaska.

Johnny on his first calf just before he
whizzed by and kissed the post.

The day I was a real cowgirl. That's me on the left
We were looking for stray cows.

A real Eskimo dwelling, that is made of whalebone and skins. Garry and Denise in front of door.

My first and last dog sled ride.

Jim and I found our first nugget while panning near Girdwood, Alaska on Labor Day weekend, 1950.

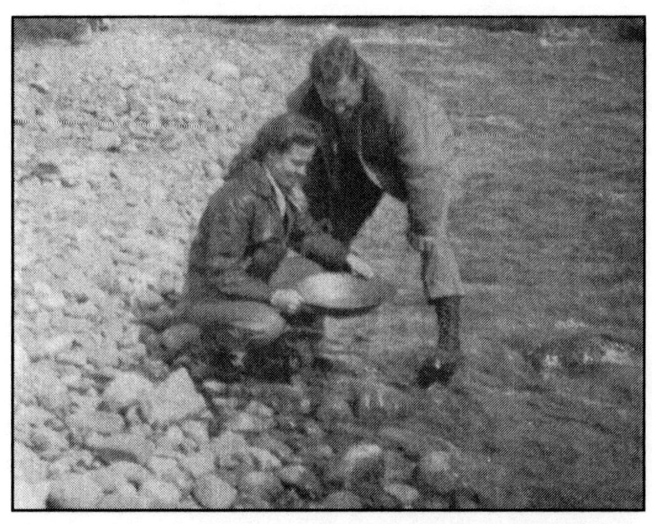

That's me on the far left. I was watching Bob on the far right with glasses. We were all going panning.

James D. Edwards and Annette Alderson
Married November 15, 1951.
Both brothers said that I shook so much,
there was nothing but stems when I
threw the bridal bouquet.

Garry pushing Denise around in the snow.

Do you think Denise is understanding everything Garry is saying?

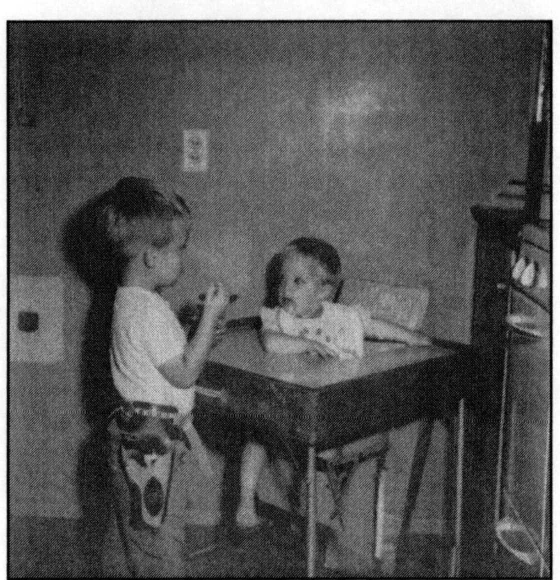

Chapter **17**

The War Ends

My family and I thought we would lease a store near the shipyard gate. Mom and I left our tacking skills to the other women that were helping defend our country. We would concentrate on feeding the hungry ones that passed by each day. Everyday I would go to town in our dilapidated truck to get five pounds of loaf meat that this handsome butcher would slice for me and a five-pound loaf of cheese which was sliced.

Due to the war you had to have government stamps to buy some kinds of food. I don't know why some of these things were rationed. Bacon was one that took a stamp. "Girls, I always got my bacon without a stamp."

I know this guy's name but I can't spell it. He would wrap the bacon up and put it with my meat and cheese. This young black headed butcher liked me. I was a little hesitant in going with him as he asked me many times. He always wanted me to meet him at the store. I figured if he couldn't pick me up at my house, I wasn't going with him. So I didn't. And too, I had male friends that came to my house. He and his family were Lebanese who owned this store.

When we came back from Alaska in 1947, I went to Pascagoula to visit Mom and Dad. Mom and I went to a restaurant for lunch one day. As we were paying our bill, this good-looking butcher walked in. He saw us at the register and came over and gave us a big hug. He said, "Katie, your daughter would never go with me. Where have you all been?" I told him we just came back from Anchorage, Alaska for the winter and we would be heading back next spring. We talked for thirty minutes or so, and our paths never crossed again.

"Oh well, I thought you girls may like that little tidbit."

Every night Johnny, Mom, Dad and I would sit around the dining table in an assembly line fashion and made sandwiches for the next day. We made sandwiches out of all the meat and cheese. We bought twenty-five pies each morning. We cut each pie in seven slices and wrapped them, ready for the pick up. We had lunches ready for people to pick up or they sacked what they wanted. We had five of these old fashion iceboxes full of all kinds of drinks. We sold out every day. Mom would go to the storeroom to fix lunches for the late comers. We sold groceries and anything else that people needed. We were in business. As soon as the whistle blew that ended their work day, Dad, Johnny and his friend, Travis Gibson, were there to help out. It took the three of them selling drinks as fast as they could pick up a bottle and get the top off.

I'll never forget when President Roosevelt died. The whole country seemed to come to a standstill. The war was still going on hot and heavy. It was announced over the radio April 12, 1945 that our leader had died in his fourth term as president of a cerebral hemorrhage.

During these war years, as I have said above, lots of things were rationed like gas, shoes, sugar, typewriters, some cloth materials. Oh yes, I knew a manager of a cloth store and I got material whenever Mom wanted to make a dress. And also that good ol' bacon that I would get each week was rationed. These things that were rationed were used for war purposes. In what way I just don't know.

The war ended September 2,1945 and peoples lives were taking on a new dimension. We let our store go back to the owners. Dad and Johnny stayed with the shipyard and Mom started restaurant work. I began working on the next chapter of my life. I prepared to further my education at Draughns Business College in Jackson, Mississippi in the fall of 1945.

As soon as the war was over and this ration stuff lifted, I ordered a typewriter from Sears. I went to the shoe store and purchased a couple pairs of shoes. I want you to know I was twenty-two years old and stepping around here in "high cotton". When my typewriter arrived, I took it out of the box and immediately started punching the keys. I just couldn't get the thing to type. Now this is the first time I had ever touched one of these things. I set back and studied my newly arrived typewriter for awhile and decided to take it to our young minister's house. I knew Jimmy Cogswell and his wife, Peggy, could fill me in. I put my typewriter in the car and headed for their house. Jimmy answered the door, took the typewriter and put it on the table. He said, "What's your problem, Annette?"

I asked, "Jimmy, how do you ink this thing?"

I could see he had a smirk on his face when he pushed a button or something on it and he started typing. I thought, whoa, smart thing, that typewriter. At the same time I had ordered a book to teach me how to type. Soon after this encounter, Jimmy and Peggy Cogswell were sent to China as missionaries and we started corresponding. For the first two letters he would ask me if the typewriter needed to be inked again. I thought, smart alec, just stay in China, and see if I care.

I don't know why so many of my friends and families were going back to the areas they came from. Perhaps due to the war being over the shipyard wasn't going to make as many ships, so people left. Dad and Johnny stayed with the shipyard until we left for Alaska.

The time came for me to go to Jackson, Mississippi to enter Draughns Business College. This is where my typewriter came in handy. Why I chose a full course I'll never know. I hated school and I figured I'd never work in an office, but here I am sailing off in a completely new direction. My life is full of new chapters. This is one I could hardly wait to get to the last page. "Ole'" Annie, just had to pay for a full course that would take me over a year to complete. If I had paid by the month I could have quit anytime I wanted to. Within my first two months there, Mrs. Osgood sent me off for a job interview. This business was going to pay me thirty-five cents an hour, so I didn't take the job. This wouldn't have happen if I paid by the month. Since I paid in cash they were trying to kick me out of school. The next day I went back to school and took my seat.

Class started and the first thing after roll call Mrs. Osgood looked at me and wanted to know if I was going to take the job. I told her thirty-five cents an hour wasn't enough. She looked me square in the eyes and before the whole class said, "Well Annette, I'll tell you one thing, you defense workers will have to come down to earth." She rambled on for awhile and then flopped herself back in her seat in a huff. I leaned over to the girl next to me and said, "Her ol'man must not have cuddled up to her last night and she is taking her frustration out on me." I wondered if this is the way people were treated when they paid in full. That taught me a big lesson. Never pay in full up front.

I had a room in a big house that was stuffed full with fifteen girls about my age. It was two to a room and one room had four noisy girls. We all had fun. Halloween of 1946, six of us painted our faces, and put on wigs and silly clothes and headed for town. We came by some road equipment with their small trucks parked and decided to let out about half of the air in two tires. We saw a guard approaching so we took off. Now I know this wasn't right but we really didn't do any damage. We were having some girl fun. We came to the Toddle House and thought we would stop and sink our teeth in one of these special waffles. "Girl's, do you remember those delightful waffle houses? You dropped your money in a dispenser just as you went out the door."

Oh well. We went to the water faucet that was at the back door to wash our hands before we went in. One of the cooks came running out to see what we were doing. When he found out we were washing to come in for a waffle, he invited us inside to use their wash basin. As I was drying my hands in the hall, I looked up and saw a friend sitting at the counter. She said with a wave, "Hi Frances." She always called me by my old name. Now we were supposed to be in disguise. We went around to the front door to enter and took our place at the counter. I sat on the stool next to Frankie. She was one of my girlfriends from Pascagoula, Mississippi.

I asked her, "Frankie, how did you know me with all this garb on?"

She came back with, "Frances, I'd know you anywhere."

The girls lingered extra long with me so Frankie and I could catch up on lost time. I knew she was in Jackson but I didn't know where. From then on we kept in contact.

I got a part-time job at a place called National School Pictures. It later became full time work. I worked on the enlarger making 3 by 5 pictures. I liked my bosses and this started me on my way in photography. I like to think I helped Jim Whiddon and Don Garrett in their beginnings in the school picture business. I was with them on Amite street in an old three-story frame building when they first started out. We were already in a new building before I left for Alaska. I went back to see them in 1995. Jim Whiddon had passed on. Before we started our tour through the plant, Don told my friends that were with me about the parties we had back then. He looked at me and said, "Annette, the year you left, we started having fewer parties. Things were changing so fast. We were in most of the states making pictures. The plant had enlarged so much, that put little time for fooling around."

Don said they sold the business for several million dollars a few years back. It was great seeing one of my old bosses that dated back fifty years. I worked in photography for years and loved every bit of it.

"There were a lot of happy stories I could tell while I was

there."

One day after work Jim Whidden rented a truck for a trip. We went miles out of Jackson. We were in someone's woods that Jim knew. We roasted wieners, told stories, and just laughed and talked till midnight, then we headed back home. We would go on short trips. Jim and Don would give us an evening on them about ever third Saturday. We were always celebrating something. We worked hard and were rewarded. I think Jim and Don liked to party as much as we did.

"While I'm still here in Jackson I'll tell you when and why I drank my first glass of wine."

Now mind you I was twenty-three years old. About six of the girls I worked with at National School Pictures made an appointment with a lady that read tea leaves. Our boss, Jim Whiddon, took us by the hotel, where the tea leaf reader lived. We really wanted to ride in Jim's new Studebaker.

Just as we were walking up to her door, one of the girls leaned over and asked me if I would keep her purse. I said okay. I don't know what she was afraid off. I guess she thought I was the brave one. We were invited in and given a cup of tea to drink. She talked to us as we consumed the brew. Then she proceeded to "read" the tea leaves in each cup. As she read my leaves she leaned the cup over and said, "You see these two leaves that are crossed? You are sitting at a table drinking wine with three other people." By that time I looked at two of the girls out of the corner of my eye. They could tell I didn't believe one word she was telling me. I have never drank anything intoxicating in my life. With this little event finally over, Nell and I headed for home. I told her that since I had never in my life tasted any of the alcoholic drinks, I would just have to make this happen. Well, I did.

I called my boyfriend, George, and told him to get some wine. He said he would have to go across Pearl River and get it from a bootlegger. Now George worked at the police station and

I had him heading to a bootlegger for a bottle of the illegal stuff. Nell and I took four small glasses. Now I just couldn't go out drinking with just George and me. Nell and Tom went with us. We went to this club and parked outside. Would you believe I didn't want to go in because I had never been in a club before, either? I told Nell to keep me straight. I had no idea how I was going to act. Those three people thought this was funny. I told George to come on and he poured my first glass of wine.

We started sipping on the juice and my head started swimming. I was already sitting close to George and my long hair was hanging over the back of the seat. I started giggling and wanted to know if this is how a person feels. Nell would say, "Frances straighten up now and quit giggling." I would ask for another glass of the stuff. Nell would say, "No George, she's had enough." By that time the whole bottle of the bootleg wine was gone. That was the worse tasting wine I have ever had. I thought, never again. It even had a bad smell. I didn't know any difference then. I can look back on that outing and I don't see how we drank the mess.

At one time my two girl friends and I dated three baseball players that played on the Jackson Senators team in Jackson, Mississippi. After every game we went out for a steak dinner and they made me learn to drink beer. Jerry said, "Annette, this is one thing we do after every game." I said, "Okay, bring on the steak and beer. The steak I can take, but beer?"

"Okay girls, I did learn to drink the stuff, but I had to force myself."

Bettie said, "Yeah, now we know how you were made to like the stuff. I'm sure you were able to hold your own in that line."

"Okay, knock it off now, let's go on to another subject," I said as all three of them were looking at me with smirks on those silly faces. I wondered what they were thinking.

I met and became friends with Virginia Hunt at Draughns.

I don't know why she suggested going to Alaska when we finished school. There were government jobs open there. I could hardly wait for Saturday to roll around. That weekend I took the first bus heading for Pascagoula. When I walked in the house the first thing I said was, "Mom, I'm going to Alaska when I finish school." Jimmy heard me say this and came out of his room with one of his unpacked duffel bags on one shoulder and a heavy parka draped over the other shoulder and said, "I'm ready sis, when do we go." Jimmy had just been discharged from the Navy and he was ready to start traveling again.

Chapter 18

Our First Trip to Alaska

While I was finishing school, Mom got her pen and paper in hand and started writing to Washington DC. From there she started getting letters from Fairbanks, Juneau, Anchorage, and Palmer. All were Alaskan towns and cities. We knew what we would have to do. The last letter we got was from Anchorage, Alaska. In it she was told that if we weren't good pioneers for us to stay home. Now that raised the hair on that little lady's neck.

I graduated from Draughns early 1947. I slapped my diploma in my handbag, went to work and told my boss, Jim Whiddon, I was sorry but I was quitting my job and heading for Alaska. Jim knew I was leaving as soon as I graduated. I went to my room in the house I shared with fifteen other girls, packed my clothes in my trunk and suitcase and I was settin' on go. I called Dad to come get me.

That night the girls wished me well on this great adventure, which they thought was all talk, and we said our good-byes. That morning I hugged my roommate, Nell, goodbye. Dad was waiting for me in front of the rooming house. We loaded my trunk and suitcases on the truck and we headed back to Pascagoula. It seems funny how you can stay in one place for so long and make good friends and the next minute you are gone, never to see most of them again. I wrote to my roommate up through the middle 1950's and finally that petered out.

When I arrived back at home base, Mom had sold the furniture and kept what she thought we would need to supply our new home in Anchorage. Some of our friends helped us load our one and a half-ton Ford truck. They didn't think we would get any further than Forrest City, Arkansas. The people at church didn't think we were serious. We did go to Forrest City to see Pearl and Lynn before heading north. When Lynn saw what we were driving to Alaska, he was speechless.

He managed to say, "Katie, you are not going anywhere in that truck. You will go to Memphis tomorrow and get a new one."

They took our old truck and car to Memphis the next morning and traded them in as a down payment on a new two-ton, dark blue Chevrolet truck. On their way back they stopped at a lumberyard and bought plywood and a tarp. Dad and Lynn began the next morning making the back of the truck livable. Not bad traveling for these little "chigger ridge" hillbillies. We did take three mattresses and enough furnishings to set up housekeeping once we arrived at the other end of our journey. While I was in Jackson, my family put in a small theater in Vancleave, Mississippi, about fifteen miles out of Pascagoula. Mom ordered the film from New Orleans, Louisiana and would show movies on the weekends. We closed it down and took our two movie projectors with us. We thought if they didn't have a theater in Anchorage, maybe we could put one in. We had boxes of the things we would need. On top of these boxes we put three mattresses. The men would sleep on top of the boxes and Mom and I would put one mattress on the floor of the truck for our bed. This would be our home for who knows how long.

We hated to leave Pearl behind, but after wet eyes, hugs and good-byes on July 18, 1947, our goal was set on the great north, the last frontier.

"Remember girls, we had never been any further than Memphis, Tennessee, Little Rock, Arkansas and Pascagoula, Mississippi. I went to Fayetteville, Arkansas and the school trip east. I guess Jimmy and I were the only members in the family that traveled more. After all, he spent several years in the Navy. This was stretching our wings a little, don't you think?"

We were brave little souls going through country completely unknown to us. But what a thrill it was. We had each other and maps in our hands. Dad drove and Mom kept him company. Johnny, Jimmy and I stayed in the back. Now this truck had a tarp for a top, and plywood sides with a door in the back. We made a sign that said "To Alaska or bust" and we would put it on the back door as we drove through small towns.

Then we would take it down and wait for the next town. Some people would drive up to the side and talk to us, then as they drove past Mom and Dad they would say, "Good luck on your way to Alaska." When we eventually stopped for our noon nourishment, Mom wondered how did they know we were going to Alaska? When we came out of the cafe, she happened to look on the back door of the truck and saw our sign. Our Mom was a good scout and she usually shared our foolishness.

We thought Seattle, Washington was where you crossed over into Canada and from there to the Alcan Highway. I can not bring to mind ever having a map on how to arrive at the beginning of the Alcan. Surely Mom had one somewhere about her. We got to the Canadian border and that wasn't the right one to get to Dawson Creek. They sent us to Idaho Customs to cross over at King's Gate into Canada.

Washington State is beautiful. We stopped at the edge of some little town about nine o'clock one night dog-tired. We saw a sign that was perched on a hill that said rooms for rent. Dad stopped the truck and we all piled out. Dad was trying to get the boys to go and see if the motel was open. They didn't want to go, so they were standing there arguing about who was to go when a highway patrolmen drove up and wanted to know if we needed help. Dad asked the patrolmen if it was permissible to park on the side of the road and sleep in the truck. He said it was okay, just pull over anywhere. So we did. We had it arranged where we could make two very comfortable beds. We spent many nights in the back of that truck.

When we arrived at King's Gate Customs, where we crossed over into Canada, we had to show the amount of money we had, also we were to have spare tires, an extra gas tank, and tools. We started taking our money out to show them our worth. When they checked Mom and Dad, the custom officer said, "Your Mom and Dad have enough to get you guys to Alaska.

They also said we were the first to come through going to Alaska from Arkansas. We really came from Mississippi, but we had Arkansas truck tags.

We had no idea the Alcan opened for public travel the year of 1947. The Alcan was built for military use during the war. Of course, people that lived in Alaska could travel over this road. Brother Jimmy said Mom must have told them we were homesteading in Alaska. We were there, if I'm not mistaken, and traveling on it the same month it open. I saw this on some Alaskan Alcan History on TV. Why did we choose this year and month to travel north? Come to think of it, they might not have let us through if we were any earlier. Now that is just a guess. Seems like we were in on many early beginnings. To start with, we were the first to leave the hills on Route Two in our community in 1942, except the guys that went in service. Now we are among the few that made their way north over the great Alaska Canadian highway, later known as the Alcan.

We journeyed through Banff National Park and saw our first bear. When we stopped for a better look the thing came right up to our truck. Before the bear made footprints on the truck Dad drove off. In places like this, bears beg for food. We threw the animal a bite to eat out the back as Dad began driving off. Banff National Park was beautiful. That was the first big park we came to. Believe me our eyes took it all in. Who would have thought of seeing an outside swimming pool in Canada? I guess us kids thought anything north of the U. S. was frozen over. I wish we had spent more time there. But we had bigger things pressing on our minds at this point in time.

We would stop along the road and prepare most of our meals. The back of the truck became our home for ten long days.

We spent the night in Edmonton. Remember Dad had to get this extra gas tank put onto our truck. We stayed in a hotel that had a nice cozy bedroom with two beds and an "inside toilet". We visited many little outside "johns" along our trip. It was a real treat when you had inside plumbing. Johnny, Jimmy and I thought we should give Mom and Dad some time alone, so we went downtown to a movie. Before the movie began something came on the screen and everybody stood up, so we popped up. We didn't know what for, but it was a tribute to their Queen. After the show, we stopped by a little coffee shop and goofed off for another hour before going back to the hotel. Oh well, we always managed to give our parents their space in all of our travels. We usually stayed in the same room when we found two beds in a room. Mom and I occupied one and the boys and Dad the other one. We were a conservative little family. Everyone paid their own way. We bought our own food for we knew what we could afford. Each one of us anted up twenty bucks for the truck kitty. When that was used up, Mom would stick her hand out for more money. Mom and Dad weren't bashful about this little matter. Each one of us paid our own way, right on down to the gas and oil.

We left Edmonton with two full tanks of gas and several quarts of oil. We restored our food supply, filled our two big jugs with Canadian water and off we drove into the unknown. The days were real, real long, and getting longer. I began to wonder if we would ever see Arkansas, our own natural state again. It got where you didn't see anything on the road. No buildings, gas stations were far apart, like one or two hundred miles apart. Now you see why the extra gas tank. There were emergency shelters along the way, which we did use a couple of times. If you used the wood that was in the building you had to restock the supply for the next person. You really looked out after yourself and the next fellow on the road. If you saw a person stopped along the road, you always checked to see if they needed help. Who knows, you may be in trouble and need help. As far as I could tell everybody was so glad to see people, that they would stop just to talk.

A beautiful lake came in view that would make a great place to rest for lunch and maybe a nap. We took our time. My brothers and I got off to ourselves and talked about our great plans we had for the future. All of this big talk came out of the hills with us when we left Arkansas. But I must say the talk got a little bigger as time went on. After a lengthy rest, we saw the folks putting the gear back in the truck. We knew it was time to move on. At this time in our travels we didn't know that bears would attack you if food was available. We were fortunate not to be encountered by any of these rowdy creatures.

We could tell Mom was getting a little blue about this trip She wondered if we had made a mistake in this wild adventure. Mom and Dad drove, while me and my siblings piled in the back. Fifteen or twenty miles up the road Dad stopped. We got out to see what was going on. There poor Mom was sobbing her head off wanting to head back to Mississippi. We hadn't made it to Dawson and she threw this bomb on us. They alighted from their seat and Dad got the old coffeepot out, started a fire and got the coffee brewing. By now that pot was beginning to show its age. You can't remove black from the pot very good with river water. We did use the lakes and rivers to camp by when we came to one. When Mom returned to a good frame of mind, Dad said, "Okay, kids, let's get started back to Mississippi."

Mom said, "Oh no, why do you want to go back to the states?"

By now she had forgotten it was her idea to start with or was she trying to wiggle out of it? Now Mom could be a little cagey. Dad winked at us and we piled back into the truck and headed deeper into the northern territory.

We continued taking enough time to enjoy the beauty that was forever looming around each mountain and in the clear streams we could cup our hands in and bring up a cool refreshing drink. Maybe jump in for a dip before retiring for the night. Were Jimmy's and my dreams really coming true? Would we really get our car one-day? To this day I've never bought a car by myself. I've always had one, but Jim, my husband, would always be with me when one was chosen. There are really three Jim's in the family. My husband Jim, Daddy Jim and brother Jimmy. Early dreams do come true. We've always wanted to travel, so at last here we are in the middle of nowhere, and we don't know what would confront us around the next mountain.

Chapter 19

The Alcan Highway

The government built the Alaska Canadian Highway in 1942, mainly as a military supply road. Later it took on the name "Alcan Highway." They started road construction at Dawson Creek going toward Fairbanks, and from Fairbanks on toward Dawson Creek Finally the road met and they called that connection, Contact Creek or Contact Point. It amazes me how they could go through all those grizzly looking mountains, cut and hash their way through and meet at that one point, probably right on time. There was a war on, you know. Of course, our first trip over this road was the original dusty gravel road built for military use. It had lots of crooks and turns. They were forever working on this road because of the frost upheavals. I believe most if not all of the Alcan has a blacktop on it now. The Alcan stretches 1,523 miles and goes from Dawson Creek, British Columbia to Fairbanks, Alaska.

We finally came to Dawson Creek and the first milepost loomed in sight. These posts would mark our way each mile from now on. We had a brochure that told us where all the lodges and gas stations were by the mile post guide. If it said there was lodging and gas at milepost 333, you would find it at that post. All of these places were small when we first went through. As the years went by the towns began to grow in size. Today nothing is the same as it was when we traveled the Alcan in 1947. It was all a delightful new experience for the Alderson clan.

"Girls, here comes Jim. I'll try to keep him here until I'm through telling you about the plane that flew eye level with us," I said as Jim came and sat by me.

As I have said, we did take our time along the road. Dawson Creek was a hundred or so miles behind us now. It was a new adventure seeing the milepost every mile we drove. I have not mentioned it before but we did see a lot of wild creatures in this vast wonderland. It's very silent here. No animal sounds, just road, mountains and trees. If you really want to be alone just come and sit yourself out here in the middle of nowhere.

We met Mr. Johnson, one of the men that worked on the road and was there when the two roads met at Contact Creek. He showed us the certificate he and the others received for working on this unusual stretch of road. The war brought on a lot of new beginnings. The Alcan made it possible for the lower 48 to communicate with the last frontier, so here we are with wide smiles stretching across our faces admiring this awesome country.

Oh, there were mountains to go around and over, and we saw many deep canyons. This was enough to scare the living daylights out of you. Remember, my fear of heights. One day around noon we were winding around one mountain on this narrow two-lane road and to our right was this very deep canyon, and lo and behold a plane flies up beside us. We could see him moving his mouth and Mom started smiling and yelling at him. Of course, no one could hear exactly what the other was saying. A few minutes later he waved and turned around and headed back to where he came from.

We stopped at every town we came to. We would eat at one of their cafes and rest for awhile before continuing our journey. I'll never forget one dinky cafe we stopped at. We ordered hamburgers, fries and drinks. The lady didn't put onions on our burgers. Mom asked for a slice of onion. The lady said she didn't put onions on hamburgers. She said they sold a lot of onions but not on hamburgers. Now my brothers and I were just about to crack up. Mom and this lady continued their conversation. Mom asked, "Can I buy a slice of onion?" That did it. Johnny had just taken a drink and he spewed a mouth full of liquid across the table. Jimmy and I couldn't contain ourselves any longer. The woman walked off in a huff. Mom says, "Can you believe that. That little heifer won't even sell me a slice of onion." Poor Mom was really set on onion that day.

We drove late that night. Mom and Dad were asleep in the back. The boys and I were in front putting in a few more miles before we stopped for the night. I was sitting in the middle and half asleep. I could hear the boys talking but it didn't make any sense. As you well know when you are half-asleep you don't hear things just right. They said something about a railroad crossing coming into view and I came up from there yelling, "Stop the truck, a train is coming." Jimmy slammed on the brakes just before he drove across the tracks. That liked to have pushed us through the windshield. Shook Mom and Dad up some, too.

Jimmy hollered, "Where?"

When I became completely awake, I told them that I thought I saw the lights from a train and it was bearing down on us. What I did see was a car coming alongside the tracks. Dad started banging on the back of the cab and told us to stop. Of course we obeyed. Dad asked, "What is going on with you kids? Katie, we better take over before these kids kill us." Instead of driving on we pulled over to the side of the road and slept the rest of the night.

"Sounds like you guys had a ball. Would you travel the Alcan today if you had the chance?" Alene asked. "Yes Alene, I think I would. Nothing is the same now. The population of Anchorage is as large as Little Rock. I understand that it has built up a lot along the Alcan. But yes, it would be a new experience that I would enjoy."

We eventually arrived at Customs at Tok Junction. The place where we checked in, to leave Canada and enter Alaska.

When we checked in the ranger wanted to know if we saw an airplane along our way. Mom has always been a good talker, so she spoke up and said, “Yes we did. One flew beside of us as we were winding around on one of those steep mountains. He flew beside us for awhile and then turned around and left.”

“Mrs. Alderson, you people were two days late getting here and he was checking to see if you were in trouble,” he said as Mom was searching for something to further this little confab.

Dad filled the gas tank, checked the oil and filled one of our water jugs. He brought the jug in and set it down on the floor before he paid the bill. We all left the premises at the same time. No one thought about the jug of water. Mom continued eating her sandwich as we left this checkout station.

There was a shorter way to Anchorage if we wanted to take it. It would save many miles but the road was narrow. If we took the main road going to Fairbanks, when you reached the Y, you would have to double back to Anchorage. So we turned left and drove the shorter route to Anchorage. That did save many, many miles of driving.

Around one of these mountains we almost ran smack dab into a bear and her two cubs as they were laying in the dusty road. I was sitting in the front seat with my parents when we saw this bear knock her cubs up this steep mountainside. Those cubs rolled up in a ball and when they stopped rolling they stretched out and were out of sight in no time.

The road was so narrow it started Mom sobbing again. I think Mom was concerned about our safety. We were in a territory and heading for a town we knew nothing about. On this road there was no way for a car to pass, unless you or the other car backed up to a wide spot made just for this purpose. We met no one and I believe the road was at least a hundred or more miles long. I could be mistaken on the mileage. Our first lunch break on this narrow, dusty road was really a trial. First off we missed our water jug that Dad never picked up when we left Tok

Junction. We wasted no time here. We ate our sandwiches and continued our journey. I don't know why Mom was so unhappy but she kept on crying. Maybe it was because we left her oldest daughter back in Forrest City. She never told us her problem. We finally arrived at the main road that went from Anchorage to Fairbanks. We turned left and headed for Anchorage. We sat in silence and enjoyed all off this beautiful wilderness. Arkansas and Mississippi were so far away that we didn't stop for one minute to think about the distance.

In 1947 Mom had just turned 47 years old somewhere between Dawson Creek and Whitehorse. I got a picture of Dad sneaking up behind Mom and putting a handful of chipped ice down the back of her blouse. Mom let out a squeal that the dall sheep could have heard on the highest mountain. We enjoyed the time we spent along the Alcan. At this time in our travels we didn't encounter any of the wild animals. We didn't know the bears would sniff you out and demand their share of food. We always enjoyed our lunch and rests period along the Alcan.

Chapter 20

Our First Cabin in Anchorage

We were told from the letters we received from Alaska that housing was scarce in Anchorage. So when we came to Palmer, we saw a sign saying cabins for rent. We rented one and this became our first home for two weeks. We knew we would be fifty miles from Anchorage. We knew we could handle this drive until we found a place in Anchorage. The owners of these cabins were some of the people that came up on a government deal back in, I believe, the late twenty's or early thirty's. The government wanted people to come and farm that area. The government would furnish everything. They showed us their first home they dug back in a bank. They gave us lettuce and potatoes right from their garden. The lettuce was so juicy it would almost squirt out of the side of your mouth. Potatoes were the same way. Everything grows fast in Alaska with the long days they had. We put dark coverings over our windows until we settled elsewhere and had our own larger living quarters. The sun would be up as early as two or two thirty in the morning. The men and Mom hired on with the Railroad. "Ole" Annie stuck with photography. I could have made more money if I had followed the family in government employment. I'm still not sorry I followed the photography industry. I have met some mighty nice people in this line of work.

About the second week as we rolled into Anchorage heading for our jobs, a man flagged us down on the outskirts of town. We stopped. His name was George and he said he wasn't trying to stop us but if we needed a place to stay he could fix us up. Girls, the old boy wasn't just waving at us, he was hoping we'd stop. He was building some cabins and, of course, he needed customers. He nabbed us because we did need a place closer to work. Palmer was two or more hours drive each day.

George had a cabin almost completed. He would flag anyone one down that looked like a newcomer to Anchorage. I know, we saw him do this a couple of times. Dad and the boys helped George make our cabin livable. They roofed it with a tarp. We would cook our meals on a little wood stove. Dad made a frame for two regular size bunk beds. While I made the top bunk up for myself, Mom put sheets and covers on the bottom bed for her and Dad. Dad and the boys put boards on the rafters and placed a mattress there for these two little jug heads sleeping quarters. I was hoping they wouldn't forget where they were when it was time to get up.

Mom backed off to one side and stood there admiring this work of art and said, "I can tell you one thing, they can't accuse us for not being good pioneers." Mom was proving her point.

I was up early one morning heading for the coffee pot, when I heard voices above me saying, "Look out below." By the time I looked up I had two pillows in my face. Dad said, "You kids cut that out and get ready for work. We'll be leaving in fifteen minutes."

George even put a tarp up for the door. How nice, Ha! "I can tell you girls one thing, this Alderson clan was living in high society now, right?"

Bettie commented about our arrangements that were made in our little Alaskan cabin. "Wasn't that a little small for five people?"

"Yes it was, but we always gave our parents plenty of space," I said putting my writing material aside and tossing a few things around that won't be printed in this book.

"We were all grown. Each one of us needed our own freedom. Maybe that is why we got along so well together. No one really questioned where we were or what we were doing."

Most of the time we would discuss, in front of them, where we went.

After about a week in this cabin, my brothers and I thought we'd go to the 4th Ave Theater and enjoy a good show and give Mom and Dad some quality time together. As we walked out the door Jimmy said, "Dad, we will be back around eleven o'clock. Don't wait up for us now, you hear." We gave Dad the old thumbs up and winked at him as we walked out. Now Mom wasn't watching us doing our little antics.

This is the first time we took in the nightlife in this fair town. You had a big choice of bars and clubs to choose from. I think that first night we tried them all. Not in drinking but just seeing the insides of many! Needless to say we didn't go to the show and we weren't home at eleven o'clock. What the heck, the days were long. This is all new stuff to us little country yokels.

Shipcreek Grocery was downtown on 4th Avenue. We would stop by pretty often to get a few staples. One day we were parked across the street while Dad went in to fill his grocery list. Dad walked out of the store all humped over with two full sacks in his arms. He knew we were watching him. He saw a young lady coming his way. He perked up and tried to tip his hat when something made him fall in the middle of the street. I mean groceries went everywhere. The lady bent over and asked him if he was hurt. Dad said, "No ma'am." She walked on while Dad crawled around collecting his goodies. We laughed so hard the whole truck shook. Dad did look funny crawling around in the middle of the street.

My brothers worked at the Alaska Railroad and later that week they were sent out to work on the railroad tracks. The railroad tracks are something they always kept close check on. They would have room and board somewhere down the line. Finally it came time for them to take the train to their destination. We knew that when we saw the first snow on the mountains we could just about guess when it would come down to our level. So Dad says, "Okay boys, come the first snow, we are leaving for the lower 48. Be here now, you hear me?" "Yes Pop, we hear you. We'll be here."

Sure enough about the second week in October we saw the first snow on the mountaintops. When it came to the tree line, you could no longer see how far down it was getting. We knew it would get to us anytime. Where the boys were, was a different story. It was already snowing on them, and they were very anxious to get home. That afternoon their boss came in riding one of the little rail cars. The first thing Jimmy and Johnny did was to make their way to their boss and reveal the sad news. Jimmy told him that the family was heading back to the states with the first snow and they had to get back home. Their boss told them he'd take them into Anchorage the next day. Of course Jimmy and Johnny were having a fit to leave now. Their boss told them he had a little business that needed attention. After that he would take them back to camp to collect their clothes and then on to Anchorage. So they rode this little rail car back to civilization.

About midnight we heard whispering outside and someone trying to get in our tarp door. Dad asked, "Boys, is that you?"

They said, "Yeah Dad, let us in, we can't get this crazy flap open."

All of this commotion woke Mom and me. This brought on a lot of why and what for's.

Dad questioned, "Why are you boys here? Did you get laid off?"

"No Popsy, it snowed where we were and you told us you were leaving out at the first snow fall. We see it didn't snow here," Johnny said with a grin.

The boys continued their work at the railroad shop with Dad until the first snow in Anchorage. We quit our jobs. I went to the bank and withdrew all our money, which I had in my name. We regrouped and backed the truck up and started loading up once more for the long trip back home. We never used our movie equipment. We were told no one was allowed to put a theater in this town. The richest man there had everybody "buffaloed" and no one cared to call his hand. It sure wasn't in our thoughts. This rich man, I have long forgotten his name, was later killed by one of his own coal cars at his mine.

Chapter 21

Preparing to Return to the Lower 48

Dad stopped by the liquor store and got a pint of liquor. At the beginning we didn't know he had this with him. We knew he wanted to stay in the truck because he placed our boxes ever so neatly. Johnny finally got in and started helping in a more hurried fashion and in the process covered his bottle. Poor Dad. With the job accomplished the boys and I took our place in the back. Mom fussed at Dad a long way down the road. Finally Dad pulled over and got out and told one of the boys to drive.

Dad said as he was getting in the back, "Maybe she has cooled off enough to stop that fussing. I wonder when the bee stung her?"

"Now Dad, remember your bottle that Mom didn't know about? We saw you sneak a drink. She smelled the liquor on your breath. You can hide your bottle from her but you can't hide the evidence. She always has her own way of knowing. Now Dad you know that. Why didn't you share it with us? We could have mixed up a little warm toddy for the road," Johnny said as Dad climbed in the truck.

"Girls, do you really think our Dad would have shared his bottle with his kids. I think not. We were really joking, or were we?"

Liquor has hurt many members of my family. Mom hated to see Dad misuse it. She saw how it hurt her brothers. When I was growing up I wondered why a person couldn't take a drink and stop at that.

We told Dad it was going to get a little cool here in the back going through Canada.

Dad said, "There are quilts here so cover up more."

As we checked in at Tok Junction, the first thing Mom wanted to know was if they found a green gallon jug of water.

The ranger reached behind him and retrieved a jug from the shelf and handed it to Mom.

"Mrs. Alderson you were pulling out when we noticed it by the counter. I sure hope you had another jug with you," he said as he handed her the necessary papers for the other end of our journey. The men grew beards in the four months we were in Anchorage. They thought that was "cool", coming out of Alaska with a grizzly looking beard. I must say that facial hair was not becoming to them. Later, after the family in Forrest City saw their beards, Dad, Johnny and Jimmy headed for the bathroom and started shaving this growth off their faces.

In Canada we stopped at one of the emergency shelters to rearrange the boxes that were put so hastily in the truck. This was Mom's idea. Of course Dad did most of the work. In the process he was really looking for his bottle. At last he let out a wild yell that echoed throughout the canyon and held up his bottle and said, "Hey, I found it." Drinking was one of Dad's worst habits that Mom wished so many times he'd quit. I snapped a picture of him when he found his bottle. We got everything put back in a more comfortable fashion.

From that time on we made very few stops until we hit Sweetgrass, Montana. We have made many trips over the Alcan Highway and it never got shorter. You just kept the "peddle to the metal" until you reached your destination.

Somewhere between Tok and Dawson we pulled into a small place to refuel. It was dark. I mean black dark. This gas station had no lights at the pump. It seemed like these little businesses used a lot of flashlights on the outside. There would be a light at the entrance but at the pump it was a different story. I'm talking about 1947 now. Come to think of it, we may have been their only customer that night.

"Remember girls, the days were getting much shorter and plenty of darkness was surrounding us on our long journey homeward."

Dad and Jimmy stayed in the back of the truck while Mom, Johnny and I took care of the gas. The attendant was paid, and Mom stood there and talked to him and his wife for awhile.

Johnny and I were just standing at the back of the truck passing time with their son. The young guy started to lean against the truck gate. Johnny swiftly said, "I wouldn't do that if I were you."

Dad and Jimmy realized what was about to happen, so they were prepared for a little fun. About that time Dad put both hands on the guy's shoulders and kinda dug in.

The guy jumped away and asked, "Whoa--whoa--what's in there?"

"Well, we have a gorilla back there. If you provoke him he can get mean," Johnny said as he touched the gate.

Dad and Jimmy heard him questioning this so they started shaking the truck. Dad got where the guy could dimly see his eyes and he growled like he thought gorillas should sound, while Jimmy continued shaking the truck. They figured this guy had never crossed the mountains to see what kind of world was on the other side. So they played this up pretty good. Now Mom was still talking to this man and his wife and she knew nothing about what was going on back of the truck. After a thirty-minute rest Mom said it was time to hit the road. When Mom settled in she asked us what was going on back at the truck. Johnny told her the man thought we had a gorilla back there.

Mom says, "A what! I can't believe you kids."

"Well Mom, he seemed to enjoy the story," Johnny said putting the truck in high gear and whizzing on down the ghostly dark road at probably forty miles per hour. We drove a few more miles before we heard a knock on the inside cab window. Johnny pulled over and stopped. We all piled out ready to stretch our legs for awhile. Dad said he needed some sleep and he couldn't while the vehicle was in motion.

So far, no snow, and it was really nice out here under the starstudded sky. Just gorgeous! In a few minutes we heard something overhead making a swishing sound and as we looked up the beauty just floored us. You can't imagine how picturesque the northern lights are until you see them in all their gracefulness, fanning out across the sky until it reached it's fullness, in a fantastic array of bright, soft vibrant colors. You could talk in low voices and be heard clearly yards away. For once in our lives we were in total silence, except the faint sound the northern lights made as they danced across the sky. I felt like I was completely surrounded by God's presence. I don't know how the rest of the family felt, but I actually stood in awe at His marvelous handiwork. We finally made our beds and fell asleep. Would we, this feisty Alderson clan, want to make this trip again in 1948? You bet we would!

"Hey, you guys don't fall asleep on me now." I said as Della's head began to lower a bit. "If I get boring let me know. Since you gals are here, Jim is not showing up as much. He can see I'm in good company so he won't interrupt and make me lose my train of thought as I continue my story."

At dawn I felt Dad crawl across the foot of my bed and retrieve the gas stove, coffee pot and breakfast materials. Later, I smelled the aroma of coffee as it perked and drifted toward the truck. I can guarantee you Dad was not to far from the door for fear a bear would amble upon the odors of the bacon cooking. We got up one at a time rubbing our sleepy eyes. Dad handed each of us a cup of the strong java as we approached the cooking area. He turned the fire up on high and hurriedly finished our breakfast. We needed to make tracks before a bear got the whiff of our breakfast. We learned that they will sniff you out and demand their share. This was early morning and still pretty dark. We ate in haste, and got the equipment loaded back in the truck.

As we were pulling out, Dad saw a black bear heading our way. Now sweat started pouring from his face. His foot hit the gas a little harder and we were gone. The bear turned toward us and tried to catch up to what he thought would be a good meal. After that little scare we made sure we parked in clear areas. That would give us time to see if there were any animals in sight. We were not fooling around much now because of the weather heading our way. Not knowing what a Canadian winter would be like, we just kept our gas tanks full and continued pushing our way toward the U.S. Customs.

We checked in at the U.S. Customs at Sweetgrass, Montana in late October. We rested a bit. Then we decided to drive long hours until we reached the Willis' home in Forrest City, Arkansas. After all we did have three drivers. Somehow Dad didn't want me to drive. I have never seen Mom drive, until she bought her first car. I hated to sit in the middle. Remember how they made the windshields? They would put a metal strip down the center of the glass. I would always have to lean my head a little to the right or left to see the road comfortable.

We didn't tell Pearl exactly when we would be there, but I can tell you one thing, when we did arrive, it was great seeing her. You could tell she was concerned because of the distance that separated us. We walked around sniffing and wiping the happy tears from our eyes for awhile before we began informing her of the fun stuff we had done. She would have loved being with us on this wild adventure. We stayed with her and Lynn for a week then we headed back to our old familiar grounds.

They dropped me off at the rooming house where I stayed before leaving for Alaska. Most of the girls that I thought I'd never see again, were still there. My roommate, Nell, was glad to see me. I got my old job back at National School Pictures. That name, I believe, had been changed. Mom and Dad headed for Pascagoula, and my brothers found jobs in another part of Mississippi. Where and what they did, I long forgot. We had driven thousands of miles. You get in a car and distance is nothing.

We knew a hurricane had hit Pascagoula and the surrounding areas right after we left in July heading out on the first leg of our northern trip. It was amazing the damage it did to the coastal area. I had never seen anything like it.

Chapter **22**

New Orleans Mardi Gras

After a month of doing nothing, Mom and Dad saw an ad in the paper where they needed help in Venezuela, South America. They drove to New Orleans to inquire first hand about what kind of work this was and maybe sign us up. It would be with fruit of some sort. They had lodging for singles but housing wasn't ready for married couples. That put a stop on that real fast. Mom wasn't about to let us go by ourselves. Really, that was smart thinking. They stayed in New Orleans and looked around for a few days. They came across a small eatery for rent. I can just see a smile spread across Mom's face. She could write checks on my brothers and me. Right then we became partners with our parents in this small eatery called "Eat Good Cafe."

"Now how do you girls like that name. That should bring in the hungry ones, don't you think?" I said.

"Here comes Jim. I think we need a cool glass of wine. Maybe some of my home made rice saki," I said. "Good thinking Annette. I know where it is, I'll get it," said Alene as she headed for the kitchen. Alene is good at serving us. After all she is the youngest in our group.

"Were you there for the Mardi Gras?" Bettie asked.

"I sure was. My friend, Nell, and I got a four-day weekend off to go to New Orleans for this event. I'll never go to another one. There were so many people attending this gala you could hardly get anywhere.

There was a rooming house next door to the cafe. Four young men came down from Minnesota and roomed there for this festive occasion. They ate all their meals at the Eat Good

Cafe.

Of course, when Nell and I arrived they were the first people we met. Now don't think for one minute that Nell and I had one dull moment. With those four young men and my two brothers, we had a ball. One day on one of our outings Nell leaned over to me and asked, "Frances, (she always called me by my old name) I wonder what people think when they see six men tagging along with us?"

I said, "I don't know but I bet they wish they were in our shoes."

We went dancing on a riverboat, I believe the name was Queen Mary, does that sound right? Or the Delta Queen. I have long forgotten the guy's names, but one of them and I waltzed all over the dance floor that night. He could waltz better than anyone I have ever danced with. Oh, how smooth and graceful he was. We would go on the riverboat, to a show, and to some of the clubs, then we would enjoy the parade that came in front of our cafe. There was enough going on that we had to make a choice. Millions of people were there, or it sure seemed so. Our cafe was right on St. Charles Avenue. I wonder if they still use that avenue for the parade? We went downtown for something that was going on one day. There was such a crowd you could hardly move. Needless to say I'll never grace this festive event with my presence again. Never, and I know that is a big word. That is the largest crowd I have ever been in to this day.

Nell and I needed to head back to our jobs at National School Pictures. There were no vacancies on the bus, train or planes. We called Jim Whiddon, our boss, and told him of our predicament. He said come when you can. So we really had two more days at this huge celebration. I was twenty-four at this time and I thoroughly enjoyed this. But I still won't go to another one. So many thousands of people were frightening. I had heard about Mardi Gras for years and wondered what it would be like. Now I know. In spite of the huge crowd, I still enjoyed every moment of this yearly event, and I still say never again. Once is enough.

It was time for these young northerners to head back home. They told Mom if she trusted them they would take us to Jackson, since they were going in that direction. So we loaded up and headed back home. Those guys were great people to know. They were big farmers with their dads and as each one got married they continued writing to Mom. Especially when anything new would happen in their families. Mom and all four families exchanged Christmas cards every year until her death. So with this ride, we finally reached home and work. Our money was running out. The girls at work, were all over us and wanting to know what this big Mardi Gras was like. It's amazing how by 1948 people still didn't venture very far outside their own little shell. People I knew still didn't travel much.

"Girls, it came time when this beautiful northern territory was nudging once again at our heart strings. As the month of July was taking shape, Mom called to see if I was ready to hit the Alcan once again. She knew I was getting antsy and settin' on go."

Johnny wanted to see Priscilla, his Pascagoula girlfriend, before heading north. This was on a weekend and Dad told him not to stay in Pascagoula long. He was to come by Jackson and pick me up on his way to Forrest City. Johnny got in his car that evening at dusk and headed out on the shortest route.

There's no telling where his mind was because the next thing he knew he was sailing in thin air before he hit the water. Not knowing how deep the water was he opened the door and jumped out. Apparently it wasn't too deep because I don't think the car was under the water. There was no sign saying the bridge was out. So there Johnny was in pitch darkness, wringing wet. He remembered seeing lights somewhere back up the road, so he started walking. He finally came to a house with lights on. He bravely walked to the front door hoping no dogs were around. He knocked and this person opened the door and saw him dripping wet. I'm sure Johnny did some fast talking that time of night. He was invited in to use the phone. He called the police department and they came and got him. When they arrived at the Biloxi police station, he called Priscilla and wanted her to come and get him.

Her dad realized something was wrong so he took the phone and said, "Boy, what is going on here. Where are you?"

Johnny told him he ditched his car in the river and he was at the Biloxi police station.

Mr. Shanks, I believe that was his name, said, "You stay there, I'll be right down to get you."

So he drove to Biloxi, Mississippi to get Johnny, Which wasn't to far from Pascagoula. Johnny was mighty glad to see him.

Mr. Shanks had his wrecker to get the car out of the river the next day and brought to his garage to get it in shape for the trip north. Johnny called Mom in New Orleans and told her what happened.

Dad got on the phone and said, "Boy, meet us at Pearls. You promised your friend in Forrest City you would do some welding for him before we leave for Alaska. Are you okay?"

"Yes, Dad, I'm all right."

After spending a couple of days with Priscilla, Johnny rode the bus to Forrest City. Dad sent Jimmy to Pascagoula to help with the repairs.

When the car was finally dried out, repaired and ready for the trip, Jimmy came by Jackson to get me. We thought we would make a little detour to see some of the Alderson and Littlejohn relatives in Oxford, Mississippi before heading to Arkansas.

We were looking for Peggy Bailey, one of our cousins. Someone told us her boy friend was a butcher at the meat market across the street. As we entered the market, Jimmy asked the butcher that was cutting meat, "Say, do you know where we can find Peggy?" Here comes this guy with a large knife in his hand.

Jimmy said, "Hey, I'm Jimmy Alderson, just a cousin and this is my sis, Annette."

I think Jimmy was getting a little nervous with that knife glaring at him. The guy kinda laughed and told us where she worked. We walked in the store just as Peggy was getting off from work. We recognized one another instantly. We had met a year before when Dad wanted to see some of the Littlejohns and Aldersons. As Peggy, Jimmy and I were making our way across the street, she spoke to a man as he passed us.

She looked at us and asked, "Don't you know him?"

Jimmy asked right back, "No, who is he?

That is Ernest Littlejohn, your uncle."

Jimmy ran back and stopped him. After some good conversation with Peggy we said our good-byes and I haven't seen her since. Uncle Ernest took us to his sister's house, which was where he was staying at the time. I had seen Aunt Nanny many times before and she was the only Littlejohn that I really knew. Uncle Ernest knew we were going through Memphis and wanted to know if we would take him by his daughter's house. We said we would, so he packed an overnight bag and we were on our way.

We stopped about ten miles out of Oxford to meet one of Uncle Ernest's daughters. That woman wouldn't let us leave until she prepared a dinner for us before we started our long trip to Memphis. She fixed us a meal that was fit for a king in nothing flat. I thought, man what talent, if I could cook like that I'd get me another Eat Good Cafe and just stay put. Just as we were entering Memphis, Uncle Ernest wanted to know if Jimmy and I drank beer. We said we did, so we pulled in at the first decent bar we came to. Come to think of it, I bet Uncle Ernest had visited this bar before. We were enjoying a good talk about our Littlejohn relatives. We knew very little about this side of our family. All of a sudden two men started fighting at the far end of the bar. Those men went round and round and they suddenly stopped when they saw the bouncer coming toward them. They put themselves back in their seats and ordered more beer. We didn't know what they were fighting about but now they seemed friendly. Uncle Ernest looked at me and said, "I'd better get you guys out of here. If your Dad knew I had you two with me in this place, he'd probably punch me in the nose. We got up and left. There weren't a dozen people in this place.

We arrived at his daughter's with our smelly beer breath. Uncle Ernest's wife had been dead for many years, and he was dating a lady that his daughter didn't like. He thought he'd pull one of his jokes on her. Before we went in, Uncle Ernest said he was going to introduce me as his girlfriend. I said okay, "What the heck. I'm used to this kind of stuff."

This went over like a lead rock. You could have sliced the air with a knife. When I got my uncle by himself I said, "What have you done to me? She won't even talk or look at me and you told her I was her cousin." She didn't believe us. We didn't stay long at this "ice house." When we got up to leave, we hugged our Uncle goodbye. I whispered to him, "This is going to be a hard one Unk. You got yourself in this mess now dig your way out."

I hoped he and his daughter made up before the night ended. He and my Dad were a lot alike. That was the last time I saw Uncle Ernest Littlejohn.

Chapter 23

Our Long Journey Back To Alaska

Jimmy and I finished our journey to Forrest City late that night. The next morning Mom told us that Aunt Blanche was going with us. We thought, the more the merrier.

Dad went downtown to be with some of his old buddies and have one last fling at shooting craps. Well, Dad came out a loser. Right then Mom took control of his money. Of course, my brothers and I laughed at this. Poor Dad, going to Alaska and all he had in his pocket was cigarette money. We immediately changed Dad's name to "Grubstake." Eventually he became known as "Grub" or "Grubby". The name finally went with him to his grave on November 19,1980.

We went to Memphis to get Aunt Blanche and to say goodbye to Aunt Virgie. We came back to Pearl's for a few more days. We hated to leave her behind. There seemed to be thousands of miles between my only sister and me. Now Mom had one sister left in Memphis, and a daughter in Forrest City. We had lived close all our lives. Once again we were parting. After many lingering hugs that July, 1948, we got in our vehicles and left on another long trip to the last frontier. Pearl turned and started toward the front door. You could tell she was sobbing. Mom's cheeks were wet. Me, I have been pretty good at hiding my feelings, but my heart was crying out for her to come along with us. That was the last time I saw my sister alive. That ended my contact with Forrest City. I had aunts, uncles and cousins there that we would see on our visits to the states but no one really close. My brothers and I became closer. In Anchorage, Johnny and I would hit the clubs on Saturdays, and Jimmy and I would go to church on Sundays.

"Girls how do you like that combination?" I asked not really wanting a reply.

I know we went out a lot together, but we still had our girl and boy friends. I sure didn't want my brothers tagging along with me on a date, unless they had a date. Johnny and I did double date once in a while.

"Now I ask you, have you ever seen such a contrast in what I did? Now don't misunderstand me. Johnny and I did nothing bad. We enjoyed our Tom Collins and danced till 12:00 midnight. Bob Hope once said that Anchorage had the longest bar in the world. He was right. You went to a club, stopped in at a bar or you went home. Card games were big and poker parties were on a roll. Once a month we had this poker party at our house. I could never win and I wasn't about to lose much of my money so I became the server of the snacks."

Oh well, back to my story.

Dad collected the $20.00 from each of us for the truck kitty and handed it to Mom. He didn't expect money from Aunt Blanche. He knew she was running on a shoestring. Dad, Mom and Jimmy piled in the truck, Johnny, Auntie and I in the car. We tooted our horn and waved one last time, not knowing what that wave really meant to my sister and headed our very small caravan north.

We went by Kansas City, Missouri to see cousin Jerrie and her family. While there Jerrie gave Dad a very thin yellow nylon shirt. The next day of our journey we stopped to gas up. At that time, 1948, they had gas attendants to serve you. The guy checked the oil and water and put gas in both vehicles. When Dad got out to pay the man, I couldn't believe my eyes. Dad wore suspenders under this very thin nylon shirt because he wanted to leave his shirttail on the outside of his pants. Girls, this was a sight for sore eyes. Dad had hooked the suspenders to his colorful boxer shorts, and his underwear was pulled up to his neck. We started laughing. The attendant looked to see what we were laughing about and he started in. Dad looked to see what was so funny. When he felt his back he realized what he had done. He hurriedly paid the bill and got in the car with Auntie, Johnny and I.

He started off with this kick, “You all could have told me before I got out of the car.”

“Hey Dad, we didn’t know the fix you were in until you got out to pay the man,” Johnny said, and as he looked back he saw Dad shaking with laughter.

Dad also, liked a good laugh. He figured we’d never see that guy again, so what the heck.

We stopped in one town and parked the truck. Then all six of us got in the car and drove around for awhile. We went in one grocery store to buy supplies before we arrived at Sweetgrass. Everything in Canada was higher than the states, so we stocked up. We knew we would be camping along the road most of the time. Then we went to a filling station for gas. The attendant stuck the nozzle in the gas tank and left it running for he knew it would cut off when full, and proceeded to clean our windows. There was no such thing as air conditioning back then and we had all four windows lowered. When Johnny saw him coming with the glass cleaner he rolled his window up. When it was clean he rolled it back down. This went on all the way around the car. Dad was on the right hand side of the front seat. He didn’t roll his window up and the man didn’t know it so he squirted Dad’s face good. Dad just looked at him not saying a word. Then the man started to wipe the window, but instead of the window he hit Dad’s face. That man almost lost all control right there. Of course, my brothers and I cracked up with laugher. Aunt Blanche enjoyed the fun and laughed with us. Mom was busy doing something else and she didn’t know what was going on. Mom handed the attendant the money. When he went for change, she turned to us and asked, “Would you all tell me what's so funny?"

Relating it to her wasn't near as funny as the way it happened.

She asked, "Jim, why didn't you roll the window up like the rest did?"

"Katie, he was at my window and squirting me before I knew it. So I wanted to see what he would do next."

So there you go. Later on Mom caught on.

"Bettie, you look sleepy. Should I quit for awhile?" I asked. "I'm about half way through and I have a lot more living to tell you about. So when you guys get tired listening to me, let me know and I'll fold this up until tomorrow. You did say you would be here didn't you?"

"Yes, we will be here. But don't fix us anything to eat. I'll bring bar-b-que sandwiches. Alene and Della will bring salad and desserts. So now you are off the hook. It is getting late and time for me to go. I see Jim closing the shop door, so girls we better get," Bettie said as she and the rest got up to leave.

We said our good-byes and Jim and I walked into the house. He and I were both tired. We ate a light dinner and talked over the day's events.

"Little Missy, have you gotten your fill of writing yet? I can't believe you are going to really finish this. You have a long way to go," Jim said as he started getting ready for bed. "I'm tired and I'm sacking it. I'll have coffee ready when you get up."

Before going to bed I sat at my desk and thought back on the time we left Dad stranded somewhere in Kansas. All you could see for miles around was wheat growing in the fertile soil. I've never been so tired of driving on long straight roads where all you could see were wheat fields. We were getting tired and certainly ready for a stop. After miles of driving, the crew in the truck pulled in at this station that had a hamburger bar. Auntie, Johnny and I turned right and stopped beside them. After riding for so long, you do get a little stiff. We were always glad to get out and stretch for awhile. Jimmy got out of the truck and headed for the outhouse at a pretty swift pace. "I didn't think I'd make it in time," he said, as he rejoined us smiling.

In those days we visited many of these outhouses. Some were pretty fancy with the two-hole job. I bet those outhouses were some of the first public restrooms. Oh well. We entered the snack bar area and put in our order. We were getting pretty hungry so even the greasy french fries tasted good. We asked Aunt Blanche how did she like traveling with us so far. She said it was great and the further she got from Memphis the better she liked it. I couldn't blame her. Her life wasn't easy there.

After we filled our stomachs to last for another five or six hours, it was time for us to regroup and see who rode in which vehicle. Dad and Johnny said they would get in the back of the truck because they wanted to sleep. When we got ready to leave, Jimmy looked in the back of the truck and saw a head. So he locked the back door, and went around and got in the cab with Mom and drove off. That left Auntie and me in the car. That was fine. We went a good fifteen miles or so when a car drove up beside us. I looked over and saw a man beating on the side of the car he was riding in. Lo and behold it was my daddy. His eyes were as big as silver dollars that seemed to be stuck out on little pipe cleaners. I just kept driving and talking to Auntie.

I said, "Auntie, I wonder how he got in that car?" We thought it was funny. Of course, my Dad didn't think so. You could hear the man that was driving, laughing so hard he could hardly stay on the road beside us.

As Dad was beating on the side of the car he yelled out, "Don't you want me? Stop the damn car!"

I answered back, "Well, yes I do."

That was tops for Auntie. I thought she would die of laughter right there in the middle of the ever-growing wheat. As I pulled over and stopped, Dad got out hastily and got in the back seat of our car. The man turned around and headed back to the gas station.

Dad made a quick comment, "I can't believe you all would run off and leave me. And Katie knew I didn't have a damn dime."

All of this was funny enough by itself, then Jimmy and Mom stopped and got out of the truck. We pulled up behind them and you should have seen how big Mom's eyes got when she saw Dad in the car with us. She could see the back door was still locked, but still she thought that somehow he fell out of the truck. All five of us were prodding Dad along to tell us what happened back at the gas station.

By now Dad had settled down enough to tell us his side of the story. He first wanted to know why we left him at the gas station.

"Pop, you said that you and Johnny were heading for the back of the truck to get some sleep. Now Dad, I looked in and saw a head, so I locked the door and we took off," Jimmy said shuffling his feet on the gravel.

"Katie, if you want to get rid of me just give me back my money next time. Don't just leave me with nothing," Grubby said shaking his hands in an unusual fashion. "I could just see myself working in the wheat fields. You can look out across the fields and you can hardly see the end. It's not like the cotton fields in Arkansas, where you can at least see the end of the row."

When Dad thought he had riled Mom up enough he started telling us what happened back at the station.

Katie, before I went to the truck, I thought I'd better head for the outhouse. Johnny and I left you guys sitting at the counter. The next thing I knew, you were driving off. I grabbed my britches up and ran out but it was too late. I hollered but it was no use. I was going to flag a ride but there were no cars on the road. You boys would have laughed if you saw me pacing up and down in front of that station. After awhile an insurance agent drove in and I told him that you guys ran off and left me and I needed to catch up with you. I offered him any amount of money he wanted. He said, "Let me get my insurance money first and we'll go and catch them."

I said, "Man, they are going to Alaska and I need to catch up with them now before they get any further." "Okay, get in," said the insurance man. I got in and he wasn't going fast enough for me. I asked him if he could go faster. He did speed up some. When you finally came in sight, I said, "There they are."

"We rode side by side until you finally stopped. That's the story up until we caught you." You could hear the man laughing as he turned around and headed back to the service station to collect his insurance payment.

Dad turned to me and said, "I don't believe you didn't stop when you first saw me. You all thought you could run off and leave me out here in a no-mans land with no money."

"Well Grubby, you did look odd riding along beside us," I said.

From that time on, whoever he rode with, Dad would get the keys and put them in his pocket. He told us that we wouldn't leave him again in the middle of nowhere. I do believe Mom reached in her pocket and handed him ten dollars and aughingly said, "Well here, Jim."

This money keeping was nothing new. Mom always kept most of his money. It's hard to tell events as comical as they really happened. The expressions are the funniest. By now you would think Dad would be a little nervous about going in these little outside buildings.

The next day we stopped somewhere in Montana at another gas station with the usual eating area at one end. After the truck and car were serviced and our meals finished, we started to our vehicles. Now mind you, Dad had the truck key in his pocket. He reached in the truck cab, got his pliers and headed for the outhouse. He told us he wouldn't be long. After about fifteen minutes we heard him yell.

Mom said, “One of you boys better go and see what’s going on. He may need help.”

Johnny said, “I’m not going, Mom. He doesn’t belong to me. He’s yours. You go check on him.”

Auntie was forever sitting on the sidelines, waiting to see what would happen next with the clan she so eagerly joined up with. Stuff like this never went on in her family.

We just stood beside the car gazing at the outhouse wondering what we should do. A few minutes later Dad came out holding the pliers up and yelled out, “This damn thing won’t bother me any more.”

He came toward us holding a bloody tooth with his pliers. Dad had started pulling his own teeth long ago. We had no idea he had a toothache.

He still had the tooth and pliers in one hand when he reached into his pocket with the other hand to get the keys. His eyes got big. We thought, oh no, the key fell in the hole. Dad felt in the other pocket and stopped and shook his head.

Mom asked, “Jim, did the key fall in that hole?”

After a little more searching, Dad smiled and said, “Fooled you didn’t I.”

Chapter **24**

My First and Only Cattle Drive

We arrived in Sweetgrass, Montana on July 1948. The Canadians wouldn't let the travelers cross over into their country if they were heading for the Alcan. We had to wait until they had their ribbon cutting to officially open the Alcan Highway. Johnny, I'm sure you forgot this or you weren't with us. All I can recall is Mom and me, and my camera in hand to take a picture of the Mounty. I had never seen one of the Canadian Policemen before. I do have a picture of this event. Johnny, I can't help what you say, they did have some kind of celebration before customs would let us enter Canada.

So we were stranded for about two or more weeks. A guy at customs said we could camp at the edge of town. We sure had the equipment for it. Remember now, we were supposed to be good pioneers.

As time went by, more travelers joined us at the campsite. About the third day there we had nothing to do, so my brothers and I started discussing the new names that we would call our parents and Auntie. We have called Mom, "Buckshot" off and on, for a long time. Why she arrived at this name, I have long forgotten. Dad looked at us with a silly smile and said, "I know what my name is." So he's "Grubstake", "Grub" or "Grubby". Now for Auntie. She wanted to know why we called her "BB".

Johnny said, "Now that is for bird brain."

She turned on him and was about to knock his head off.

Johnny said, "Wait Auntie, B stands for Blanche so we put two of them together, and you became our little BB."

Aunt Blanche laughed and said, "Johnny you caught me

just in time. I was about to lop that head off."

"Yeah, Auntie I know. You would have gotten your jollies out of that, now wouldn't you?"

After all we were grown people and rather than saying

Mom, Dad and Auntie we would say Buck, Grub and BB. These names did stick.

Sitting around camp didn't appeal to us. Dad and the boys found work at the Alpine wheat farm or ranch. Mr. Alpine had ten thousand acres that he was getting ready to plant, all in wheat. He needed help. Mom, BB and I went back to Shelby and rented a hotel room with three twin beds in it. They were waitresses at one of the restaurants. The photo shop wasn't hiring so I just loafed around all day. Those waiting days were the only time I was ever out of a job in my single life. Mr. Alpine's sister had eight thousand acres and their property joined. Now that was some enormous wheat field. By standing on one side and looking toward the longest stretch, it seemed to bend with the earth. Just kidding. I would really hate to be put in the middle of those two fields and be told to find my way out before supper.

I can't locate my diary, but I'm sure our clan was at the new jobs for at least two or three weeks or more. The men heard that the Canadians were having their celebration that Monday. After many days working in the wheat fields, they quit their jobs. The two Alpine boys, their cousin Margaret, Dad and the boys got in the car and came to Shelby to deliver the news to us. The truck stayed parked in front of the hotel.

When they arrived, we left Dad and Mom at the hotel. BB and I joined the other five. We went to the biggest club in Shelby, which wasn't all that big, and danced until midnight. Now, we did have one or two Tom Collins. We all agreed to go back to Sweetgrass and on to the Alpines. They had an empty house on their property with a big pond nearby. We weren't ready to call it a day so we headed in that direction.

Johnny had his rifle in the car so the boys had target practice on some ducks. Duck season wasn't in, so they kept their eyes looking way down the road. Remember, you can see for miles in this flat land! I don't think there was a mound of dirt high enough to stub your toe on. The days were getting pretty long, even in Montana. After a lot of horsing around and having a good time, Margaret knew her parents were up and her dad would be firing up the cookstove for breakfast. Johnny had propped his gun in a corner in the living room of that house and we went off and left it. Years later he and his wife, Mercedes, stopped by the Alpines as they were heading out for the lower 48 to visit friends and relatives. The Alpine boys found the gun shortly after we left. They had it waiting for him. They knew one day he would be back.

The boys put the ducks in the trunk of the car and we headed for Margaret's house. Even at that time of the morning, the Fish and Wildlife folks could be on the move. As we were approaching Margaret's home, there was a car following us, or so we thought. We drove up beside one of the buildings and the Alpine boys ran to the back of the car. Opened the trunk up and grabbed those ducks and threw them in a barrel, put a lid over the barrel and set a hundred pound sack of oats on top of that. They jumped back in the car and we drove on to the house. We looked down the road and the car was still coming our way leaving a dusty trail behind it. The car passed the house.

As we were getting out of the car, one of the boys said, "Well, that's not the Wildlife boys. We were checked last month about this time but they couldn't find the ducks." Margaret's Mom had the coffeepot on high blower. That is, the coffee perked in no time flat. Perked coffee can sure smell good. You could just about ease your hunger pains with just the smell. That woman made us an enormous breakfast. We had biscuits, gravy, bacon, eggs and jelly. Oh, there was more. The table was full. Would you believe we ate it all. Now we were up all day and all night and now we are heading into the new day hungry as bears. BB and I put a few biscuits and gravy away ourselves. At that time of my life I could eat ten pounds and it wouldn't show up on the scales. I guess the skinny days have long gone.

After breakfast, Mr. Alpine sent us to round up their cows and calves to be dehorned and branded. I thought, man this is going to be fun. Me on a roundup!

I told BB, "I'll get a lot of pictures here. People back home won't believe that we were on a real roundup."

Margaret got her horse saddled. She said Blackie hadn't been ridden all year. The minute she put her foot in the stirrup, that black horse took off bucking. That girl was hanging on for dear life. Her long hair flying in all directions. We were back at the barn hollering, "ride'm cowgirl." After awhile the horse settled down and Margaret and Blackie came back to the barn. The rest of us mounted our horses and followed her and her feisty steed to look for cows that were scattered in the distant grassland. I'd ridden horses before but not on a roundup.

I don't have an inkling of how many cows were in the roundup that day. There must have been fifty or more and their calves. We got them in the larger corral and the Alpine boys would herd the cows that needed to be branded and dehorned through this skinny chute. You could tell the poor cows didn't want to give up their horns from the way they bellowed. We could smell hair as the helpless critters were being branded with the Alpine brand.

The boys made sure the larger calves that didn't need branding were put in a separate corral. After a fashion the cows were put back out to pasture.

Now for our fun. The boys took turns riding the calves. BB, Margaret and I were sitting on the top rail watching and yelling, "Hang on, cowboy!" There was a post in the center of the corral, which must be missed while riding the bucking calves. I always had my camera with me. Everything was funny at this point in our lives. Here comes Johnny on his bucking calf. His legs going in all directions. The post came into his view. He tried to get his legs looped around the calf's belly but was a little late. We yelled out, "Jump Johnny!" We thought for sure that post was going to split him up the middle. He held onto the dumb calf and received a bad hit from the post. He survived the hit and waited in line for his next ride.

The boys thought we were having too much fun watching them get roughed up riding the calves. They started hollering for Margaret and me to come on down and take our spill. They knew we couldn't hang onto the animals. All you could do was loop your legs around the calf's belly and try to get a handful of hide and hang on with all your might. We started making our way down when we saw a car coming in our direction. We decided to see what these people wanted before we made fools out of ourselves. This couple brought us news that the ribbon cutting was delayed for another four days. In one way this was disappointing. These people went on in the house and told Mr. Alpine. Shortly afterwards Mr. Alpine and his friend came out to the corral.

He asked, "Boys, do you want to stay on until these Canadians make up their mind on what they want to do?"

So Jimmy and Johnny stayed on at the ranch. Of course, I wish Margaret and I had challenged the boys with this calf riding. We felt like we could have lasted as long as they did. We'll never know. And too, we could have hit that middle post.

It came time for BB and me to head back to Shelby. Now realize the length of time we have been up with no sleep. At that time in my life it was very easy for me to be hypnotized when my eyes were constantly on the open road. In my state, I was a real hazard to BB and myself. We had thirty measly miles to go and five miles out of Sweetgrass my eyelids were coming down. BB never learned to drive. We would sing, and honk the horn. BB would hit me, slapping my face sometimes pretty rough.

Seemed like I was determined to fall asleep. I was barely going, maybe ten miles per hour. We came to a lake on the right side of the road. Finally my head went to the side. By now BB was having fits. I was heading straight for the lake, which was very close to the road. She just hauled off and socked me a good one. That woke me in time to get the car back on the road. That shook me up pretty good and I rethought my situation. I stopped and we got out and ran around the car a few times. From then on I would stop when my eyes would get heavy and make a few laps around the car. It seemed like hours before we reached Shelby. I parked in front of the hotel and went to our room as fast as I could and fell in bed around four o'clock that afternoon. I slept till three p.m. the next afternoon. That was some of the best sleep I had on our long journey through the frontier wilderness.

The Canadians finally got to the business of their ribbon cutting. We checked out of the hotel and went by to get the boys. We all met for the ceremony. I saw my first Mounted Policemen, and heard the blast of my first supersonic plane go over, but I never saw the plane. The Canadians had themselves one big shindig that day. Needless to say the travelers were lined up to continue their long journey. We said our last good-bye's to the Alpine's, and as soon as we were checked in at Customs, we began our long haul north. I can't think of too much happening at this time. With the long wait and hundreds of miles ahead of us, we just kept the peddle to the floor and commenced to push our way north.

We did stop to eat and camp out along the road. We stopped at all the towns, which weren't many. We stopped at White Horse and went into a Chinese restaurant for a bite to eat. BB, Johnny, Jimmy and I occupied one booth. Mom and Dad were in the next booth. We saw a guy across from us dipping his fork in a liquid and then putting his fork in some seeds. We asked our Chinese waiter what was he eating. The man said, "Bird seed." Next thing we knew he was serving us some of these special morsels. We were shown how to eat the seeds. By dipping your fork into the sauce, it would make the seeds stick. Then you herd the little seeds to your mouth and grab them before they fell from your fork. Just kidding. Come to find out it was nothing but soy sauce and sesame seeds. Oh, what an education you can get on the road.

We finally made it to Tok Junction and checked in. We didn't waste anytime there. We arrived in Anchorage late that day. Dad and the boys headed for the Alaska Railroad office. Mom, BB and I stopped in our favorite restaurant and waited for the men to come back. As I was sitting on one of the stools, I happened to notice the lady next to me. It was Frances, a lady I had worked with at the photo shop the year before. She and her husband had just gotten back to Anchorage the week before. They were having marital problems. He bought a house for her hoping they could get back together. No luck there, she didn't take him back. He went out in the boonys to work and that left her with the house all to herself. I told her of our predicament.

She said she had this one-bedroom house. BB and I could sleep in the bedroom and she would take the couch. We could park the truck in the yard for the rest of the family to sleep in. We grabbed that offer with open arms. This sure beat the canvas top cabin we first lived in.

Shortly after this arrangement, Mom started working at the civilian cafeteria on Elmendorf Air Force Base. Mom moved on the base and lived in the civilian quarters. Dad hired on as a cook at the railroad kitchen. They had cooks quarters. The boys went back with the railroad line crew, so they had housing arrangements. Now for BB and I. Snooks, my photo boss and part owner of the 4th Ave. Photo Shop would hire me but I had to wait until one of the girls left. She was flying back to the states in about a month.

During this waiting period, Jimmy knew a fellow that needed help making sandwiches for the base. BB and I went to see him. Sure enough we got the job but we had to be there at three each morning, six days a week. The good thing was, we were through by eight that morning. We made 3,000 sandwiches in five hours. BB and I would get up at two to be at work by three. Would you believe that when we went to work the sun was out in full force? It came time when Snooks called me in for work. I didn't hesitate but I couldn't leave my present job so fast. Snooks told me to come in as soon as possible. I was usually twenty minutes late getting to the lab. At present I was dragging in the money, but how long would it last? I couldn't hold down two jobs for very long, not with my sleeping requirements. My eyes would daily remind me that I couldn't take too much of this.

We got wind that the railroad was having a dance at the depot. The whole town seemed to show up when a party like this was on the horizon. This happened on a Sunday night. The Alderson clan turned out for this event; our first at the railroad station. Mom, BB and I had the car because we had to be at work by 3:00 the next morning. We danced and danced. I saw my 3:00 o'clock boss and his wife there. They were kinda slowing down. Me, I was dancing around in full force. It came time when I thought BB and I had better get at least a couple of hours of sleep before we faced those sandwiches. We collected Mom from the far side of the dance floor and we headed home.

Going through town we had to stop at a signal light or was that a stop sign? I looked over and saw a bar open right across from where we were. I looked at BB and asked her if she was game. She said if I could take it, she sure could. We parked the car and went in. BB and I ordered our Tom Collins' and Mom her Mint Julep. Somehow you just couldn't break that little ole southern lady away from her only type of alcoholic beverage. That is as far as Mom ever went and it was always just one.

Fifteen till three we took Mom home. BB and I headed for work. Our boss, his wife, BB and I, got around the table in our assembly line fashion and started making our sandwiches. I was on the tail end wrapping and labeling the things. BB saw I was getting sleepy. She'd lean over and say, "Frances, wake up." I'd straighten up for a short time. They noticed me holding the sandwiches up in mid air and trying to staple the things. My knees would try to buckle under me. BB took me to the wash room and almost drowned me. I was in a bad shape. I got back to the table and the boss and his wife had smirks written all over their faces. They saw me at the dance. They knew what trouble I was in.

First chance I got I told BB, "Do you see their smiles? I bet they are waiting for me to fall on my face. I'm not going to do it. What time is it now?"

"Frances, you just asked me that. We have thirty more minutes here before our job is over."

Finally, that much of the day was finished. Now I began to wonder how I was going to make it sitting in a darkroom for eight hours without falling into the machine. I really had less problems there than I did with those stupid sandwiches. I never pulled that boner again. Soon after that, I quit the sandwich making business. I never got so tired of making sandwiches in all my life. It's a wonder I still eat the things.

At the photo lab, we had a lady by the name of Mabel, that came in every day at 1:00 p.m. to dry and package our pictures. Her husband had a gold mine that was worked only in the summer months. The unbearable winter conditions would shut his operations down most of the year. With a working gold mine you know they had money. Why she thought she had to work was beyond me. She was a nice lovable older lady that brought us brownies quite often. That little lady was a great cook.

At this point in my life I had the urge to start smoking on a daily basis. Frances, the lady that developed my pictures, also smoked. When we finished printing one day and with nothing better to do, we thought we'd pester Mabel just a little bit. We got our cigarettes out and stuck a straightened paper clip through the middle and lit up. We went to the dryer that Mabel was constantly putting wet pictures on. Frances hung over one side, me the other. Mabel noticed the ashes were getting longer and longer. We knew she was eyeing us. We paid her no mind. Finally, we had barely room on the cigarette butt to hold the thing. The ashes hung out a good two inches. Finally Mabel couldn't take it any longer. She said, "You girls get your butts away from here, now."

That ole gal had force behind the word, now. She was looking for the ashes to hit her pictures any time.

When I tapped my ashes off in my hand all you could see was this wire sticking out about two inches. She looked at the wire and sat back with a sigh of relief. She knew it had to be a trick but didn't know how we did it. She did say that we better not pull any more shenanigans around her pictures again. I do believe she meant it. She was big enough to take us on two at a time.

There were four girls working in the darkroom where I was. On this particular day, one of the girls from another room sneaked her boyfriend in the darkroom where I was. We had two printers going. We had darkroom lights on when we are printing. The machines were back to back with a walk space in between. Both printers were going full speed. As I was reaching for a sheet of contact paper, something started dangling right in my face. The thing was a big spider. I knocked paper everywhere as I jumped up and headed out the door. I heard giggling all over the room. The whole force was out to see a trick pulled on ole Annie. They had this long stick with a two-foot string and on the end they had attached a fake spider. So they got a kick out of dangling the thing in my face.

I was from the old or original crew in this lab and I really didn't care about the new management or most of the girls. I was the only one from the old crew that stayed with them and the reason was, I had no other job to go to.

Anchorage at this time had one block of pavement or was it two? It's been so long ago. We worked in an old three-story frame building. The lab was on the third floor. You could feel tremors most every day. We knew that one day an earthquake would hit. It never ceased to scare us. We were forever running out of the darkroom to stand in the doorway when we felt the building shake.

Many drunks found warmth on the second floor of this building. I don't think the door to the stairway was ever locked. That probably kept many a person from freezing in the winter months. Two lawyers had offices on the second floor and if they got there first they would rid the stairway of the night sleepers.

One day at this photo shop, the girls found out I made more money per hour than they did. Seems like I'm the last one to ever know what's going on at work. We were called in for a meeting. The bookkeeper came in and started talking about what each girl made per hour. I thought, what's going on here? Why should he tell what each person's hourly wage is? I thought we all made the same in the lab.

He called the name of each person and revealed their hourly salary. When he got to me he said, "Annette gets a nickel more because she can run all the printers and the enlargers."

To me that was an insult. I could have operated the complete lab. I had spent almost two years in this place doing the same thing over and over each day. And all of this for five pennies more an hour.

Snooks and the men that owned the lab and camera shop had already sold the lab to Pete. I was growing very unhappy with the new management. I knew a man that was in business with his family in a Title and Trust Bank. That noon I high tailed it over to the next block to see Bill. It just so happened the girl that was doing the copy work didn't like it and wanted to work full time in the office. I was hired on the spot. I went back to the lab and told Pete I was giving a week's notice. He wanted to know why I was quitting. I told him I was offered a better paying job. I kissed that task good-bye. I wanted to excel in what I was doing. Why should I continue to work here and make only five cents more per hour. I had worked on every machine and printer there. I had developed thousands of rolls of film. There was no more here for me to learn.

My new job consisted of copy work for the commissioner's office including secret stuff and all the copy work for the Title and Trust. There were many days my work was finished early. With nothing else to do most days, I would lock my door and lay on my worktable and go to sleep. Bill knew I didn't have much to do. My lab was in one of the back rooms of their bar. Their office was next to my lab. Now I said at the beginning that every other business in Anchorage was a bar.

The day has been long and Jim could tell I was tired. We had a light meal, then I went to my room and prepared for bed. A comfortable bed feels so good when you are tired. I woke up the next morning with the sound of Jim calling and telling me my coffee was ready. I gathered my paraphernalia and headed downstairs to see what the noise was all about. It was my three trusted listeners. Today they will continue to keep me straight.

"Hi, I see you guys really do want me to get this finished," I said picking up my coffee mug that has my family's picture on the side.

Betty grabbed the few pages I had completed the night before and headed out the front door with coffee in hand. She told the girls to take their time. "Give me time to read this," she hollered back at them.

We got settled and I thought about what was the next biggest event we would encounter in the fall of '48. There was no way we wanted to leave our jobs and head for the lower 48 for the winter. Jimmy and I had to buy a house because no one would rent to a brother and sister. The rest of the family had lodging where they worked. Jimmy and I found a two-room house for sale, so we grabbed it fast because winter was just around the corner. With a few repairs we made it warm and cozy for the winter. We still had our little outside john that first winter.

The spring of '49 we added on a living room, kitchen and a bathroom. A couple of guys from the army base came out and helped me paint our house white. That was a cold winter. Our bodies weren't used to the extreme cold. We knew if we made it through the first winter, we could coast through the rest of the winters. My brothers and I learned to ice skate that winter. The cold didn't slow us down on what we wanted to do. We had a ball that first year we were there.

Chapter 25

Pearl's Death

Girls, one of the saddest moments of my life was May 3,1949. Mom got a call from my sister's stepdaughter, Reba Lynn, from Memphis, with news of Pearl's death. Mom could hardly talk when she called and told me about my sister's death. Immediately I notified the men at the railroad shop. I picked Mom up at the base. I could see she already had her suitcase packed. We all met in town. Dad got the car serviced. We each withdrew what we needed from the bank for at least three weeks. We went to the house and packed our suitcases, and we were on our way by noon. We had four drivers and we drove day and night. Johnny and I had the night shift. I would keep a cool wet wash cloth on the back of his neck to help keep him awake. At daybreak Dad and Jimmy would drive and Mom would stay up front with them. Johnny and I would sleep in the back seat during the day. Someplace in Canada, Johnny and I woke up with the smell of smoke coming from somewhere. When we raised up to see what was going on, smoke was everywhere. Mom was wondering if we should turn back.

Dad said, "Katie, this must be a grass fire. It should end soon. We'll keep the windows closed tight and keep going."

We came to a truck on the roadside. A man was working over a lifeless body. Through the window we asked him if he needed help. He said help was on its way and for us to keep going and get out of this mess. By now we realized we were in the middle of a forest fire. It was too late to turn back and we didn't know how long it would last. You couldn't speed up for the density of the smoke. The sun looked like an orange dangling in the sky. The day was getting darker each mile we made. This whole business seemed to take an eternity.

Dad was one worried man and believe me the family had reason to be concerned. Smoke had already made its way into the car. We began coughing. In one of our quietest moments Dad whispered, “Katie, I believe it’s getting lighter.” We let out a sigh of relief because we wanted to believe this.

After a mile or so the smoke began to grow lighter and lighter. We finally came to a lodge that was out of the smoke enough to stop for a rest and a bite to eat. We didn’t have our usual cookouts on the side of the road on this trip. There was still a little smoke here but you could at least breathe with more comfort. We found out that we had just come through one of the worst forest fires that they had experienced this century. It had started on one side and when it reached the road it jumped over and kept burning. I don’t know why Slave Lake stands out in my mind with this fire. Maybe that is where it originated. I can’t imagine ever attempting to enter another smoke-ridden road for any reason, unless it’s a life and death situation.

When we reached Customs at Sweetgrass, Montana, they didn’t believe us when they looked at our papers from Tok Junction.

The customs agent said, “I can’t believe you people drove from Tok to here in two days.”

The man called Tok Junction to see if we were telling the truth.

The agent looked at Mom and asked, “How did you all get here so fast?”

Mom answered, “We have four drivers. We’ve had a death in our family so we drove day and night.”

When we got into the U.S., we headed for Shelby, Montana hoping to find a vacancy at the hotel where we once stayed. The owner remembered us and she graciously invited us to use her facilities. We needed to freshen up a bit before we continued our nonstop trip to Memphis, Tennessee. We would only stop to eat and gas up and, of course, take advantage of those infernal outhouses. When we arrived at the Willis' home we found out Pearl had died on the operating table from a tubal pregnancy. The doctor in Forrest City never found this to be her problem. We do have some sorry doctors floating around. She had been to this doctor many times and he couldn't locate the problem.

What's sad to me is that they were getting ready to spring a surprise trip to see us in Anchorage. They had already sold both of their cars and bought a new one for the trip. That was the second time I have ever seen my Dad cry. The first time was when my twin sister died. I guess some men can truly hurt inside with no tears. When I cry I really let go.

Now it was getting where I had no contact in Forrest City. I had three uncles and four cousins there. We heard from one Uncle. So news was getting scarce from Chigger Ridge. I've seen my brother-in-law (Lynn Willis) once since Pearl's death. That was in 1963 when Mom and Dad retired from their government jobs in Alaska, and moved to Salem, Oregon. At that time Jimmy was living in Walla Walla, Washington, and working at their daily paper. Jimmy decided he wanted Dad to teach him the mill business, So Mom, Dad and Jimmy moved back to Arkansas. Dad was really happy to come out of retirement to teach his son his trade. By the way, Jimmy and his son, Mike, still operates the mill. So Mom gave a reunion picnic on a beautiful lake out from Bald Knob the summer of 1963. It had a barge floating on its cool water, which we had the privilege to use while we were there for the day. That was the largest gathering of relatives we've ever had. Lynn was at this reunion with his new wife and son. That was the last time I saw him.

After the funeral and a good visit with relatives, it was time to prepare to head back to Anchorage. We packed our car and hugged everybody goodbye and headed for another long haul over the endless road to Alaska. At this period of time in our lives, we were young and tough. We were nothing but muscle and bone and just full of energy. Mom was 49 and Dad 51 years old, which was still pretty young in my book. Neither one looked nor acted their age. My brothers and I saw to that. We took more time going back home.

As we drove back over that particular stretch of the Alcan, we saw miles and miles of destruction the forest fire caused. What a waste of trees. But apparently a burn-off is good for the land. We finally made it back to Anchorage and settled once again in our jobs. We stayed in Anchorage the next two years with no vacation. In later years my kids and I would fly out with Mom and Dad when she would buy a new car in Seattle. We would always tour the South and visit friends and relatives.

Chapter 26

Our 1949 New Years Party

Let me tell you girls something. Now you will have to use your imagination with this one.

My best friend in Anchorage was Ruby Beasley. One day at noon we met for lunch. I needed some Aqua Marine shampoo so we headed for Hewitt's Drugstore. When we walked in, this lady came over to assist us. I whispered to Ruby, "Oh no, not this one." Now that was enough to get Ruby started.

"Can I help you ladies?" she asked.

Remember girls, at this time of my life I was still stuttering some when I would get a little nervous.

I couldn't tell who the lady was looking at because she was cross-eyed.

So I said, "Do you have a dollol boller of ---?"

So help me that is how the words came out and I had to stop. By now I had grown quite nervous. I looked at Ruby and she was grinning from ear to ear. What was so funny is that it looked like she was looking at both of us at the same time. I know she couldn't help it, she was a nice person. I made another stab at it.

"Do you have the dollol boller of ----?" I couldn't get the proper words out. I have been known to do some pretty good tongue twisters. I stopped once again and Ruby and I eyeballed each other. I looked at the lady and she eyed us at the same time. Ruby really cracked up. She knew I needed help. All she would say is, "Try this again, girl." What was also funny, the woman didn't make one effort to smile. She just looked at us with that deadpan gaze and said, "That's okay honey, I know what you want." She went and got the shampoo and handed it to me. Somehow she knew what I wanted, because I have gotten my shampoo from her before. "Is this what you are looking for?" she asked. I really thought I would have to carry Ruby out of the store she got so weak laughing. When we got outside she really let go, now I was beginning to wonder about that girl. A few months later I was in Seward, Alaska and saw the same lady in one of their drugstores. As long as I was in Alaska, our paths never crossed again.

New Years of 1949 was well below zero. Jimmy and I were supposed to meet Mom, BB, Margaret, and Ray at Mom's room on the base. When Jimmy and I arrived home from work, our house was almost frozen inside. This is the house Jimmy and I bought, because no one would rent an apartment to a brother and sister. We ran out of fuel oil and we had to locate some as quickly as possible. We thought we would never find a business that would deliver fuel at that time of night. We finally got things organized and oil delivered to our house. By the time we got heat circulating throughout the house Ray, my boy friend, came by to see what the hold up was. It was almost ten thirty and Jimmy and I weren't about to take a cold shower and put on party clothes for this big event. We really thought it was too late. Mom was so disappointed when we got to her room. There we were in our work clothes.

After thinking about this for awhile, I said, "What the heck Jimmy, let's go home and get dressed to party the rest of the night away." Mom and I wore the same size clothes so she suggested I wear something from her closet. I did find suitable clothes in there. I think she didn't want us to get out of her sight for fear we may not come back. She did have her heart set on going out that night. Ray took Jimmy to his barracks to change into some of his duds. Now we were ready to party and dance the rest of the night. We started looking for a club with a live band and there were no vacancies. One hour before midnight we finally went to the Jade Room, which had room for us. This club had no live band, but it did have a jukebox. We were met with whistles and party hats. Now we were in business. We were escorted to a table behind the jukebox. We ordered drinks. My little Mom got her mint julep. Jimmy and I got up to dance and we waltzed right over to the bar and jumped behind it and sat down on a box.

The bartender looked at us and asked, "What are you all doing back here?"

Jimmy kiddingly said, "Our Mom is at the far table and we didn't want her to see us with a drink. He asked us what we wanted. There we sat on this case of Wild Turkey drinking our Tom Collins laughing and talking up a storm. We had to make this look good so we told the bartender the color of Mom's dress and when he couldn't see her let us know. He said right now she was dancing."

Jimmy said, "Well, how about a refill."

He gave us refills. Would you believe the bartender charged us for one drink. After we finished our seconds, he told us Mom was seated. We got up and started dancing over to our table.

When we sat down, Mom asked, "Where have you all been?"

Jimmy said, "Dancing, Mom, just dancing."

Ray put his arm around my shoulders and whispered in my ear, "Where did you all really go?"

I told him that when we got close to the end of the bar, Jimmy pulled me behind it and we sat there on a case of Wild Turkey and had a drink. The bartender thought it was funny. At midnight the jukebox started playing "Auld Lang Syne". From our table, everybody was dancing except Mom and Aunt Blanche. Ray and I got that New Year's kiss in. I wonder what that New Years stuff really means? Ray didn't dance too much. I don't think he liked to dance. Man this is a good time for you to hold me close and dance the night away, I thought as I laughed to myself, we wouldn't have to sneak out behind Mom's back for a tiny bit of loving. Oh, the naughty things one can think of.

After we danced most of the early morning away, someone put a dime in the jukebox and Alexander's Ragtime Band began to play loud and strong. Jimmy and I couldn't stand it any longer. We got up and started jitterbugging. We were over in a corner really getting with the program. Shortly after we started our dance, I looked around and everybody was going to their seats to watch us. You know my shyness. I wanted to quit right then, but Jimmy wouldn't let me. After all, a few Tom Collins can make you pretty brave, so I hung in there.

Jimmy said, "Let's show off a bit. We did. He slung me on his hips, through his legs and almost lost the hand grip, then tossed me up in the air. I only weighed a hundred pounds. We even made up a few steps. Those people didn't know the difference. They were already "three sheets in the wind." We had it made. When the record ended we made a little bow. That was the first and last time anyone ever applauded me. When we went to our seats, Mom was so proud of us.

She said, "Honey, everyone sat down to watch you two dance."

I replied, "Those people were all drunk, Mom. They probably had to sit down. Mom, do you really think we did a good job?"

Mom was always proud of her kids. After our New Years party we took Mom, BB and Margaret back to the base. Ray went back with Jimmy and me. After all he was my boyfriend at the time. I can't recall dancing too much with him, but I do remember us holding hands where Mom couldn't see us. Now weren't we sneaky. We had five miles to go before we reached our home. We entered our car and turned up the heat. We should have known better than that. All three of us took turns trying to keep the car on the road. It's a wonder we didn't kill ourselves that night. You have a few drinks and when you turn the heat up you get pretty sleepy. We finally got home. I have no idea how long it took Ray to get back to the base. That was a boner we never pulled again. From that time on we were very careful on how much warmth we put in the car on these very cold nights. Sometimes we would go home in a cooler car, so there.

Do you girls remember the Petticoat Junction TV show? Ruff Davis, the guy that ran the train with Smiley Brunette was in Anchorage performing at one of the clubs. Jimmy was the emcee at the club where Ruff performed. Johnny and I thought we'd go down one night and watch Ruff do his comedy act. Johnny ordered us some kind of big drink with two straws. Finally, Jimmy came out on the little stage to introduce Ruff. We were right in front of center stage and up one level. We knew he would see us. When Jimmy came out, Johnny and I scooted closer to each other and started sipping our drink at the same time. We were really trying to mess Jimmy up. When he walked off the stage he gave us the old thumbs up sign, which meant, your trick didn't work, did it?

The family had one car and we would take turns using it. Tonight was my night. My girl friend and I were going to a movie. When the show was over I took my friend home. Jimmy had just begun his new job at the radio station and I was to go by at a certain time and give him a lift home. Well, I waited out front for thirty minutes. No. Jimmy. I thought I'd better check and see if he was still in the office. When I walked into the main entrance of the studio all I could see was one man. He was sitting at his desk with his back to me. It was quiet in the whole area. I went through about five offices before I reached him. All of these offices had wood up about three feet then finished out with glass about three feet more. I didn't see any other door where I could get to him so I went in and out of these offices until I reached his desk. The floors were carpeted so he couldn't hear me approaching him.

When I reached his desk I asked, "Hey, is Jimmy here?"

The man dropped his head to his desk. I thought he fell down dead. I was beginning to get scared, because me and dead people have nothing in common. When he raised up I let out a sigh of relief.

He said, "No, he left an hour ago."

I told him I was sorry I scared him. I also said, "I guess we are even, because you gave me a scare too. Man, I thought you died on me."

The next day he told Jimmy what happened, and that he did have a heart problem.

He said, "That little woman liked to have caused my heart to stop beating."

It came time when Johnny was being drafted into the Army. He thought he'd head for Seattle, Washington and see if the Navy would take him first. That didn't work because the Army had already called him. When he returned home I could tell he was disappointed. So we headed for one of our favorite clubs, the Aleutian Gardens, for a drink and to talk over what had transpired during the week he was gone.

After a short while, the waiter brought over drinks from some unknown person. Johnny asked who sent them. He nodded in the direction of a larger table surrounded by twelve or more people. A lady stood up and bowed toward us and smiled. I knew her. She was a waitress at the Oyster Loaf Restaurant. This is where we girls at the lab would go on our breaks for pie and coffee. It was the town's favorite restaurant, the largest one in Anchorage at the time. Remember girls this was in 1949, and the town was still small. This restaurant was also only about four stores from our lab. The next day on our break, we went to this restaurant for our pie and coffee. When I went to pay my tab, Marge was at the register.

She asked me, "Who's the cute guy you were with last night?"

I sounded back with, "Oh, that was my brother, Johnny."

She gave me a quick look and said, "Yes I know, come again?"

"Marge, it really was," I said smiling as I left heading back to work.

That same week brother Jimmy and I were in for dinner and Marge was at the register.

She looked at me and said, "I guess this is another brother."

I nodded my head and said, "Yes it is, Marge."

Jimmy and I walked out hand in hand as he whispered, "Keep her guessing, Sis." Later on Ray and I went in for refreshments and when he paid the bill, here comes Marge up to the register and said, "I guess this is another brother."

I answered back, "No Marge, this is Ray, my boyfriend."

We heard her mumbling as she turned and left us, "Damn, she sure has a lot of brothers." Sometime later Mom and I went in for a cup of coffee and when we went to the register to pay our bill I looked at Marge and said, "Hey Marge, this is my Mom." She walked off laughing. I always kept her wondering because I would smile as I left the restaurant.

Early in 1950 Jimmy and I sold our house and the family got back together in an apartment in the Vets Housing. Since Jimmy was a Navy veteran, he made arrangements for the apartment. Aunt Blanche kept her room on the base. Our apartment was upstairs. My family was back sharing expenses, which made it easier for each one of us. I know I could put a lot more money in my savings.

We always bought the seasonal concert tickets that were offered during the long winter months. A violinist was performing that Saturday and we didn't want to miss that one. I got all dressed up, including heels and fur coat. I didn't want to ruin my looks by putting on overshoes. The entrance was wet but the walkway just inside the building was dry. It sure looked like it was. About my second step inside I slipped and fell on my keester. I must say it was a neat and graceful fall. As Jimmy was helping me up he almost lost his composure. I can tell you one thing, if you waited at the door long enough you would see someone else fall besides me. The thing is, living in Alaska, you'd better be able to take a few spills.

My buddy, Ruby, was leaving Anchorage and heading back to her home state, Missouri. She checked out of her apartment at the end of the month and stayed with me until her plane flight two weeks later. Johnny got the brilliant idea of the three of us going out to celebrate her leaving our fair town. We headed for the Ambassador Club. We danced and talked and had a great time. Some guy was always coming over to get me to dance with him. I always accepted his kind offer. After all, I was the third person in our party. He may have been the odd one in his party, also. It was getting late for me. I most always head for home by twelve. One thing about these clubs, there was so much smoke in these places that my eyes would get red. It made me look like I'd been out on an all night drunk. And I was getting sleepy. Remember me and sleep? I told Johnny I was ready to go home. He said, "Let's have one more drink." I came back with, "no more for me," I can take a cab home. By now this young man was sitting with us. He offered to take me home. That didn't go well with Johnny, with him knowing I had consumed more than one drink. So he made Ruby promise that she would come back with him after he dropped me off at our apartment.

Johnny let me out in front of our apartment. I walked upstairs and entered the living room. Mom was in the kitchen. For what reason I don't know. One can only guess why moms still check on their kids when all three of us were in our twenties. I said, "Hi Mom," and I headed for my room.

Ruby and Johnny circled the apartment building and decided to stay home, also. We lived upstairs in the Vet's Housing that had a very squeaky stairway. Ruby and Johnny took their shoes off before ascending upwards. They opened the door with shoes in hand and ran smack dab into Mom. Johnny stopped off at the kitchen to get a bite to eat. He and Mom were going round and round. Johnny always liked a good fuss, in fact he would egg it on. Ruby came to my room and thought it would be best for her to take up residence at the hotel. I told her that wasn't necessary, just to climb in bed, listen, and see how Johnny gets out of this one. Ruby wanted to know what happened. I told her Johnny made one big mistake, he stopped off at the kitchen. If he had continued on to his room she wouldn't have had anyone to fuss with. Later, Johnny knocked on my door and came in.

He asked, "Sissy, did Mom jump you?"

I said, "No, I didn't stop at the kitchen, either. One day little brother, you'll learn."

It got quieter during the night and everyone pulled the covers up around their noses and snored the rest of the night away.

I greeted Johnny and Ruby the next morning with a smile.

Johnny asked, "How did you pass Mom so smooth last night without her jumping you?"

"Age, little brother, age," I said, picking up my fork and wading into the eggs and bacon Dad had just cooked.

I had a couple of friends (Mary and Charles) that were always arranging blind dates for me. They were always nice guys. We four went out for dinner one evening. We talked about everything under the sun and finally they brought me home. Ron walked me to the door. We said our goodnights and he started down those squeaky stairs. I opened the door to enter the living room, when I heard him running back up the stairs. Ron was taking two steps at a time. When I stuck my head back out the door to see what he wanted, he planted another kiss on me. Then turned and ran back down the stairs. He was a good looking guy until he smiled and that ruined his handsome looks. He had this certain way he smiled. Poor fellow!

"Girls, I have no idea why guys thought they had to run back just for a quickie," I commented as I took a sip of my coffee. "Remember Ernest in Pascagoula?" I'll never understand how I could get myself into these situations. They could have lingered long enough for both of us to enjoy a little smooch. You may think that my romances with these young men were dull, but that is not so. The days or evenings were usually planned. We did a lot of ice skating in the winter months. We went to a lot of shows. There were many parties at my friend's homes. We did go to a lot of clubs to dance. The Pioneer Hall had three dances each week. We would go to the Air Force Civilian Club to square dance several times a month. "I have dated some real charmers," I said with a giggle.

I have been out with Charles and Mary many times. Most of the time they had a blind date in tow. Charles' wife was sick and in the Army hospital and I knew he and Gene were going to see her. Charles and Mary lived off base. So I asked if I could tag along. I had dated Gene before so I thought it would be okay. When we entered Mary's room she started crying. Gene and I left the room. I asked him what was wrong with Mary.

He said, "You didn't know I'm married, did you. You are here with two married men."

Now I'm mad, sure enough mad. "Gene, you nor the others had the decency to tell me you were married? How cruel."

This whole episode ended our friendship. Me being there with two married men and her sick just didn't look right. This is one more point in my life, I knew would pass.

"Hey Della, did you ever pull any boners in your young life? I guess not. All three of you married young. You can look at me and see what joyous occasions you missed out on, right?"

I told you gals I went to church most every Sunday. I would get up there in the choir and just sing my head off. I met an Air Force guy there by the name of Paul. He joined us in our young peoples gatherings many times. So, after one of our meetings, he asked me if I wanted to go to the show with him. Well, I did. We dated for two or three months then he called it to a halt. He said his wife was coming to town. Now that floored me. Him married. I thought, here I go again. A little church boy. I thought what is this world coming to. Oh well, that ended our friendship.

One day Mom and I were downtown waiting for the light to change, and, lo and behold, here comes Paul with his wife hanging on his arm. He didn't see me, so I said, "Mom, look coming here with his wife. I told Mom to just watch me. When Paul got right in front of the car I tooted the horn. He looked at me and I gave a little grin and a wave. He started hustling his little wife across the street as fast as he could.

"Now girls, they shouldn't pull that kind of stuff on me because if I get the chance I'll get'em back. You all are sitting there laughing. I know your lives haven't been all that perfect. Am I right?" I couldn't believe those three ladies just sat there and didn't say a word. I wonder what kind of story they could dig up from their past.

Chapter 27

Joining the Prospector's Society

When we went back to Alaska in '48, we joined the Prospector's Society. They rented our truck for our field trips. We would go out on the weekends during the summer months and pan for gold. We found gold in every creek, even if it was just gold dust. I still have my nuggets and what little Mom had. This year I had the jeweler to put the nuggets in a small vial and put on a gold chain for a necklace. Now I can show off the nuggets I found in the streams and abandoned gold mines in the Alaskan wilds. Jim was with me when we found our largest nugget.

We drove so high on one mountain that we got above the clouds. Now that's true. There was a narrow road leading up to an abandoned gold mine. It was really stripped out, but we had fun on our weekend adventures and always found a few nuggets in these deserted mines.

We went by train to Girdwood for a Labor Day weekend, which was a real treat. This was in the area of a working mine. The owners wouldn't let us go to the main digging area. So we worked the area down below. We walked five miles to reach the old framed three room abandoned house the females would camp in. The men had their tents. We were loaded down with our camping gear and food for three days. Everybody took their own needs. Closer to where we would pan was a one room shack where the big coffee pot was always ready for the next person to help themselves. I always liked to get in on the fresh stuff. If it sat there and stayed hot all day it would get a little raunchy. Jim and I weren't married at the time and this is one of the trips he came along with me. We found more nuggets there than any other place we dipped our pans in.

At the end of our stay, one of the men went back to the lodge and brought a truck in to take our gear out. All the women took off on foot to cover the five miles back to the Lodge. The men stayed back to load our gear on the truck and when they were finished most of them walked out. The group of women I was with bored me to near tears because they were just lollygagging around. I couldn't take it any longer. Those women walked so slow it was killing me. I was the youngest in the group so I started out on my own. I knew I needed to rattle something to keep the bears at bay. I took the cooking pan from my belt that I had my knife, fork and spoon in and started rattling it to make all the noise I could.

I had gotten so far ahead I began to get scared. I went around this big curve and I saw a long log on the side of the road. My idea was to just sit down and wait for the slow pokes. The way I was positioned in the curve, I could see a good fourth mile on each end of the road. I sat my tired body down. When I touched the log it felt warm. I checked around in a larger area. Something big had just gotten up from its nap. Now this scary stuff took on a new dimension in my life. I jumped up and started scanning the immediate area as far as I could see. I saw the bushes shaking and a bear running not far in the distance. I didn't know how far back those little ladies were. My best bet was to take off running toward the Lodge. "Girls, have you heard the song, Shake, Rattle and Roll?" That day I did myself some shaking, rattling, singing and running until the Lodge came into sight. If anyone had heard me that day, they would have wondered if there was a wild person loose in the Girdwood area.

When I walked in the door Bob handed me a cup of hot coffee. He saw me running and wanted to know what got me started. I told him my wild and spooky story as I savored my brew. I said, "Man, why didn't you give me a cup of hot toddy instead of this stuff? I'm full up to my eyeballs with coffee."

"I bet that was the last time you were caught out in the wilds alone," Della said prodding me on.

"Yes, from then on I was always with a group of people." This is the only time I can ever recall seeing a bear on one of our prospecting trips. Since I was by myself, I wonder how many people in my group believed me. I really didn't care, because if I saw another one, the people I'm with would see it, also.

"Della, I can tell you another one that stands out in my mind."

Gene, a man that Dad worked with at the carpenter shop, invited him out to show off his homestead. He lived in Wasilla, several miles from Anchorage. The next Saturday Dad thought he'd see if he could find this rugged dwelling that his friend had built so patiently out on his homestead. Gene knew Dad was coming out that Saturday. When Dad finally arrived, the first place Gene took him was to the lake where the beavers had built a large dam. Then Gene took him to see the most interesting parts of his property. Dad was invited back with his family. So the next Saturday we jumped in our faithful truck and journeyed to Wasilla.

"Now girls this all happened in '47. We were as green as gourds."

The basic elements of a true Cheechako is a person coming to Alaska for the first time and knowing nothing about what they will expect in this frontier land.

We took my friend, Don, with us. He and Jimmy had pistols. Dad, a shotgun and Mom, Johnny and I had two rifles between us. Now we were ready for bear, wouldn't you think? We got to Gene's house and he wasn't home. His wife told us to look around as long as we wanted to. That was fine with Dad. He knew his way around. We were a venturesome little clan. We left our lunch in the truck, shouldered our firearms and started walking. Dad showed us the beaver dam.

He said, " Now Katie, over in this direction is a little cabin." We kept right behind him and never came to the cabin.

He said, "Maybe it's in this direction."

We saw Dad looking around and doing some hard thinking. Johnny whispered to me, "I bet you a dollar we are lost and all we have for big game are these little pea shooters. If we see a bear we better aim at the same spot at the same time or we are in bad trouble."

My comment was, "Johnny, I think I can outrun you. A bear is not about to get me as long as I'm in the lead."

"Sissy, you mean you would run off and leave me?"

"You can bet your bottom dollar on that sweetheart. I'm not about to let a bear make a meal off my hide."

Eventually, we came to a knoll. Dad got on the high spot and motioned for us to come on up. We did. He said as sweat popped out on his forehead, "Do you see that mountain with a gorge on the side. That will be our mark to go by. We keep going in that direction."

Well, when we returned to lower ground we lost the whole mountain.

Jimmy asked, "Grubby, where did you say the mountain with the gorge was?"

We noticed a couple of moose at our far left. We knew they would attack you if they were bothered. I could see Dad sweating. That little man didn't know which way to turn.

Don was walking around with his mouth shut. We were all ready to jump down Dad's throat. He shouldn't take his most beloved family on one of his adventures and get them lost. Really, why weren't the rest of us paying attention to where we were going?

Dad went over to a log and sat down for awhile. He happened to put his hand down on the log and the bark felt mighty warm. He looked back of the log and saw where some wild critter had just gotten up from a rest. We knew Dad was concerned about our lives. We didn't have enough power in our firearms to stop any wild animal.

I saw a long line of dirt stacked up a little way from where we were sitting and I motioned for Johnny and Don. We walked over to see what caused such a mound of dirt. They had built a road and just piled the dirt to one side. Would you believe we were almost in front of Gene's house? Our truck was in plain open view. Okay, let's go back and give Dad a bad time. When we returned to where the folks were, Johnny sat on one side of Dad and me on the other, while Don listened.

Johnny started off by saying, "Dad, you should give Mom some authority here. She probably wouldn't have gotten us lost."

Dad answered back with, okay boy, don't start clowning around."

I said, "Popsy, I'm going to make the next decision on which direction we go. How many are coming with me?" Don ran to my side and said, "I'm one that will help change our course. Johnny jumped up to follow. We headed toward the long pile of dirt. We looked back and saw the others stirring in our direction. When we got on the other side of the mound of dirt we took off running toward the truck, hoping to reach it before they saw where we went.

When Dad arrived at the truck he said, "I knew where we were all the time."

Mom said, "Yes, yes, we know, Jim."

How silly can one be. These little hillbillies in bear country with nothing but two rifles, two forty five's and a shotgun.

Chapter 28

My Dog Sled Ride

I have seen the sun come up behind one mountain and a short distance over it seemed to drop behind the next one. Fairbanks has their midnight ball game each year. They did then. I guess they still do. Things have changed so much since I left Alaska. I have seen the sun come up somewhere around 2:00 in the morning and I don't know when that sucker would set. I know when it came up, because BB and I had to get up at that time to go make those sandwiches.

In time, the O'Neils sold the Title and Trust to a banker by the name of Ben. I knew they were going to sell out two months earlier. I had a girlfriend that worked in the government lab and I knew she had her own plans. She was getting married and was heading out for the lower 48. She told her boss about me, and that week I went in for an interview. I got the job but I had to wait for Joyce to leave.

During this time Ben called me to his office. He told me that my wages had to be cut because I didn't have that much to keep me busy for a day's pay. The O'Neals knew at times my work was skimpy, but they were satisfied with what they gave me. I knew all of this but I didn't want him to get the best of me so I said, "Before I take a cut I'll quit."

He says, "Well, if that's how you feel, it's fine with me."

I came back with, "Ben, I have a government job starting a week from Monday. I was going to tell you that today, also."

A week later, I kissed one more job goodbye and walked out. I patronized his bank, so I went over to his bank and changed my account over to another bank that day. Big deal, my account wasn't a drop in the bucket. I'm sure he missed my peanuts, right? When I would get my account built up to a certain amount, I'd send so much to my savings account in Forrest City. Why I sent my larger savings to a Forrest City bank, I'll never know. Mom seemed to always have her mind on her home state, and maybe return there someday.

Years later my little family and I went back to Anchorage hoping to make it our home. Jim was the flying instructor at Merrill Field. Ben had a small four place aircraft and Jim taught him to fly his newly purchased wings. One year he and his wife flew out to the states to get their two children. On their way back the plane ran out of gas just before they reached Annette Island. I guess the plane was part way out of the water. His wife and the kids got out but Ben was trapped and they couldn't get him out. He drowned in a few inches of water. The family either waded or swam to the island. He was a good pilot. He just ran out of gas. Now this is the story I heard.

I have already told you girls that I was in Alaska at the beginning of a few things. The International Airport was one of them. I was working for the Civil Aeronautics Administration, when they pushed the first tree over for this project. My boss, Walt Smith, took the first color movie at the very beginning. I was there. They made a complete color movie of the whole procedure from the beginning to the end.

While I was with the C.A.A. Walt Smith and Herman Kurringer made a group of aerial photographs of Anchorage. I printed each film as soon as the negatives were developed. When all was finished, Walt prepared an 8 by 10 foot board for this huge mosaic project. He began in the middle of the city and worked out until it was completed. It made a pretty picture of the city and surroundings.

Anchorage has expanded so much, I'd love to see a comparison of the 1950 mosaic and one now in the year 2001. What a difference I would see. I'm sure the International Airport film and the mosaic picture are still hanging around somewhere in that fair city.

I was still going with Ray. He had a friend that owned a dogsled and a team of dogs. Ray came to the house one Sunday, right after a good snow, which left over a foot of the white fluffy stuff on the ground. He told me to dress warm and put my boots on because we would be walking quite a ways. We drove about five miles and got out of the car and started walking.

"Ray, where are we going?" I asked tramping along beside him.

"It's a surprise," he said as we trudged along the trail. "When did you say your birthday was?"

I said, "January fourth, why do you ask?"

"Annette, what is today?" he asked looking at me smiling.

"It's the 4th, but where are we going in this snow?"

About that time I heard dogs barking. I moved closer and grabbed Ray's hand and hung on. Hey, I believed the wolves had spotted us. What do we do now? Looking through the forest I could barely see a house and a yard full of dogs.

His friend, Joe, was hooking the dogs up to the sled. When everything was ready, Ray and I got in the sled and Joe yelled "mush." When those dogs took off running, Joe jumped on the back runners. It's amazing how smooth the snow rides. As the dogs pulled us on the road, I noticed the cars would slow down or stop. I asked Ray what gives here? He said, "Dogsleds have the right of way and they better stop." I just sat back and enjoyed my first and last dogsled ride. I have no idea where we went or how long we were out, but it was great. Just think, all of this for my 25th birthday.

I have already told you girls about my favorite restaurant, The Oyster Loaf. Now this is back when I was working at the 4th Ave. Photo Shop in that three story frame building. On our breaks we would head for our corner booth because we liked the little white headed lady that waited on us. She always got a tip from each of us. We became very fond of her. I got to work early one morning and rather than sitting around waiting for eight o'clock I started taking down some 4 X 5 film that Snooks had developed the night before. We did the film work for the police department and also Fort Richardson Army base. That is why we always had so much work to do.

Of course, when you take film this size down you will automatically hold it up to the light to see what is on it. It was film from the police department. When I held this batch of film up to the light, it gave me the shivers. They looked frightening to me so I dropped them on the table. When Snooks came in he told me who it was. It was the white headed waitress from the restaurant that had been waiting on us for months. You could tell she had been murdered. Blood was all over her face. She and her husband had separated. He didn't like it, so he paid her a visit with gun in hand. When she opened the door he fired away. We kinda worked in silence that day.

The police arrested her ex. This is where a prison would be great in the middle of a glacier. Of course, we hoped they would hang him by his toes. This is one hanging I could have watched. She was a wonderful and kind little lady. It's a shame she couldn't have lived out her life in the happy and cheerful way she was going.

When we lived in the Vet's Housing my brothers and I met in my bedroom many times just to talk.

Jimmy said during one of our group conferences, "Sis, you just watch, you will marry a man younger than yourself. Johnny will marry a Catholic and I will wind up with a divorcee." "You know girls, that is exactly how it happen. Would you believe I'm older than Jim?" I stated as I leaned back for a little rest. "But just by two and a half months."

Mom had purchased a beautiful Oriental rug. She was so happy that she found what she wanted. You didn't dare walk on it with dirty shoes. In fact, you took off your footwear. Dad arrived home early one Friday and he was enjoying a smoke. He had become a heavy smoker by then. He was sitting there half asleep when something shook him awake. Could that have been one of those Alaskan tremors we frequently felt? He looked down and noticed ashes on the rug. Dad's eyes got large and liked to have popped out of their sockets. He checked the clock. Mom would be home any minute now. Dad jumped up and blew the ashes away and saw a burned spot. He ran to the bathroom to get the tweezers and glue and started looking for colors to match the burned spot. The area was a colorful flower. He went to the edge of the rug and pulled some matching color out and positioned it in the spot where he had put a little glue. By the time he had the spot to his satisfaction, Mom walked in. She saw the tweezers in his hand and wanted to know what he was doing.

He said, "Katie, I was trying to get a splinter out of my finger."

By now Dad was getting a little twitchy.

Mom came back with, "Well, here Jim, let me help you."

She went over to get the tweezers and Dad spoke up, " I got it out."

A year before my Dad died, November 19, 1980, we were sitting in their Forrest City home, talking over a few things before me and my kids had to head back to our house. Dad looked down at the rug and told Mom the story behind the tweezers that cold Alaskan day in 1958. He showed us the spot that he worked over so hard that day. By now it was visible. Mom thought the rug was showing its age with wear and of course, she had no idea what made that spot wear out faster than the rest of the rug.

"Ladies, do you have time for me to get Jim more in the picture? I see he is coming out of his shop. It must be lunch time."

"Little Missy, I'll go and pick up some bar-b-que sandwiches. Do you need beans or anything else to go with the bar-b-que?"

"Jim, the ladies brought lunch and I have cold refreshments in the fridge. If you want to, you can bring lunch to us."

"While we are waiting on the sandwiches let me tell you about our encounter with one of the biggest bears I ever saw," I said.

The first year Jim and I were in California, Mom came out to visit us. We showed her some of our favorite spots in the area. We were living in one of the suburbs of Los Angeles at the time. When it was time for her to head back to Alaska, we decided to drive her back over the Alcan. Jim has always been able to get a furlough whenever he wanted one. We still cooked out a lot as we journeyed the Alcan. We had an enjoyable visit with Mom, Dad, Johnny and Mercedes , Johnny's wife, and many of my old friends. When it came time to head back to the lower 48, we loaded the trunk of our car with our suitcases and food and started the long trip back home.

Jim drove late one night. The moon was out bright enough to read a book. I was already half asleep in the back seat. I felt Jim drive the car over to the side of the road and turn the engine and lights off. Then he stretched out on the front seat for a little rest. I bet we weren't there five minutes when we felt a bear nudging the car. He was on his hind legs and he meant business. He was making guttural sounds. The closer the bear got to me the bigger that sucker seem to get. Jim popped back up and wasted no time in getting the engine started. He took off so fast that he pelted the grizzly bear with gravel. As I looked back at the bear he seemed to be wondering how he managed to let his meal get snatched away so fast. We were so scared we didn't talk too much. I jumped in the front seat with Jim and held his hand for a long time. We finally came to a service station. We pulled over and slept the remainder of the night.

"Let me tell you a prank I pulled on our poor cat before we left the hills of Arkansas."

We had a loose board on our front porch and the cat was asleep on the very end. The board had a slight bend that pointed up about a fourth inch. Now I know this wasn't right, but I sneaked out and jumped up about two feet and landed on the loose board. That cat went flying through the air and landed near the big rose bush. She scratched herself out a spot, did her job, did her cover up, and went right back to the same spot and finished her nap. I liked to have died laughing at her. If cats could think I wonder what she thought. She probably thought she made it just in time.

"Annette, are you going to keep taking us back to Arkansas?" Della asked.

"I will if I can think of something worth telling. Didn't you like that little tidbit about my cat?"

"We really want to know everything about you, don't we girls," Bettie said looking around as Jim brought our lunch.

Alene went to get a pitcher of cool water. We have been here in the shade of this oak tree all day. It is really pleasant with the fresh air surrounding you.

While I'm back in Arkansas I'll tell you about our mean gander. We had some geese at one time and the gander was kinda ornery. For some reason that gander didn't like Johnny. We kids would play in the yard all day. When the gander was around, he'd make Johnny's life miserable. He'd catch that boy by his clothes and beat him with his wings. Sometimes the old critter got skin. Johnny was always black and blue. Mom either sold the bird or we had him for Sunday dinner. Poor Johnny was afraid to go out of the house.

Chapter 29

Meeting My Future Husband

"I guess it's about time that I told you girls about meeting Jim, don't you think?"

As I have said before, Mom worked at the civilian cafeteria on the Air Force base. Sometimes the cafeteria crew would make sandwiches at night. Jim was a staff sergeant with the Air Force police department. We have always had people in for dinner on special holidays. Mom knew Jim pretty good. He and another Air Force Policeman would come in at midnight, check on the employees and make sure they were safe. I kinda think their main reason was to get a sandwich. In 1950, Mom invited him and his friend out for Thanksgiving dinner. This was no big deal for me because I had met a lot of soldiers. In fact, I was dating a nice guy at the time but he wasn't having dinner with us.

They arrived. The meal was placed on the table that I had neatly arranged with the center decoration, cloth napkins and newly bought dishes, the works. I arranged the seating where I would be between these two soldiers. Who cares, my soldier and I were about to breakup anyway. I also didn't think I'd see these two Air Force guys again. That next Saturday Jim called and wanted to speak to Mom. I told him she was at work. Then he asked me if I would like to go to the movie with him?

He knew Mom wasn't home. He probably saw her at work before he called. Of course I said, "yes," that's the best show in town. He borrowed his buddy's car for our evening out. We dated ever since. We did have two theaters in town. You must remember, this is still a very small town. We dated for a year. Sometimes we would double date with Johnny and Mercedes,

Johnny's girlfriend at the time.

I had a good job with the government. Jim liked Alaska and wanted to stay longer. It came time for him to re-enlist. They told the guys that if they re-enlisted they could stay in Alaska if they wanted to. So Jim signed up for another tour of duty. Every one of the men that signed up would be sent back to the states that December. Of course that made the guys mad. They wanted to stay in this frontier land. Remember, Alaska was not a state yet. So Jim and I became secretly engaged. I didn't know how Dad was going to take this. You know, I was still his little girl. Mom knew it but I just didn't wear my ring. Jim finally talked to my Dad and then I started wearing my new diamond.

Bob, a very good friend, was really shaken up when he realized I was engaged. By accident we filled our car tanks at the same service station soon after my engagement. After we paid for our gas, we pulled over to one side and talked for the longest time. He begged me to take the ring off. I refused to do that. I said, "Bob, of all the times we have been out together couldn't you tell I was always flirting with you. You never showed too much response, and I thought I was pretty good at it. I really didn't think you cared or loved me enough for marriage. I believed we could have made the bells jingle, don't you?"

He looked at me with the softest look, smiled and said, "Yes we could, so take the damn ring off."

"Bob, we do have a lot in common. Just think of all the mountainsides we've walked on. The rivers and streams we have dipped our gold pans in. Oh yes, we could have made a great team, don't you think?" I said as he took my hand in his and held it for the longest time. I told him this engagement was too far along for me to back out now. This was a good love friendship, and I suppose he thought it would go on forever. I can look back on my life and wonder what it would have been like to have been married to a rich guy. Would I have been the person I am today? I have wondered if he ever found a woman that truly loved him. I hope so, he was really a great guy.

"Okay, you little ladies, my life has never been dull. You really don't know. Bob and I could have made sweet music together. But then you would have never known me, now would you. Look at what you would have missed," I said.

"Alene, I see the water pitcher is getting low. It's really hot here, even in the shade. Why don't you ladies run and get yourselves something cold to drink, while I gather my thoughts on this wedding stuff," I said shifting in my seat. "Do you guys want to go in where it's cool?"

Bettie spoke up and said, "No, the shade is fine for me."

"Annette, you didn't ask for it but I brought you one, also. Looks like you may need it before you are finished," she said handing me a glass of ice water as they returned.

Jim and I finally got our act together and had a military wedding at the base on November 15,1951. People lined up to hug, kiss and congratulate us. Bob came up and whispered, "I'm going to kiss you and I hope Jim doesn't knock my head off." He got my cheek. I knew Jim was sweating bullets when he walked up. Jim knew Bob liked me and he was jealous. I didn't know I married such a jealous man. We road the rails to Curry, Alaska and spent our honeymoon at the Curry Lodge.

My first small plane flight was when one of the men at the Lodge took Jim and me flying in his plane. He flew us around Mt. McKinley. We saw lots of moose and large brown bears. After a week of this honeymoon stuff, we came back home and started packing for our journey to the base in Bellflower, California. Jim wanted to fly out, but at that time I was horrified with the thoughts of flying. I knew two service guys that went down in a crash and the plane wasn't located until several years later. Oh well, Jim reluctantly agreed with me to take our first voyage to Seattle by ship. Well, motion sickness started working on me, and finally got to Jim. We eventually reached Seattle and rode the train to our designated location.

"Girls, I'm really sorry I can't say too much about Jim, because he was never around. I bet we weren't in California six months before Jim changed jobs and started riding the trains as a policeman. There were Navy, Army and Air Force policemen on board at all times because service men were always on the train going different places. He didn't tell me ahead of time that he wanted this job. He asked for and got the transfer and never told me until he was ready to head out on the rails for the first time."

We had moved from Bellflower to another suburb. Los Angeles has many suburbs and we lived in several of them.

There I sat a new bride, and a new car. I knew no one, and Jim was gone two and three days at a time. I finally found a photo lab job in Long Beach. I'll never know why I didn't get a transfer and continue working with the government. At this photo lab I met a couple that help me turn my life around. I began to realize what a real Christian should be. This was my training period, and I had better shape up. Jim was still gone a lot. We thought this was a good time for us to start our family. I wondered if I would be a good mother. I was never around kids, especially babies. In fact, I was scared to death, but too, I wanted my own children to come see me when I got old. I knew at age thirty I better start seriously thinking about a family. So here I am pregnant and Jim gone more than he was at home.

It came time for Jim to re-enlist. He had to journey to San Francisco, California for this procedure. When he arrived at the base he was told they were going to send him to Greenland. He told them about my pregnancy. They said I was too far along for the trip. Jim decided that after twelve years he'd just retire from the service. They sent him home to do more thinking before he really checked out of the service. When he went back they said, we will send you back to Alaska. With all the running around he went through, he was afraid to trust them. Jim told them he wanted out. He thought they weren't going to grant him his decision and let him out. But they did, I believe, November 19,

1953. He found a job delivering furniture. We settled in and waited for the birth of our first baby. Mom flew out of Anchorage for this event. Johnny and Mercedes had married and produced Mom and Dad a beautiful granddaughter. Now I was wondering, will mine be a boy or girl!

The morning of December 31, I felt fine. As the day began to ebb away I started feeling like I should call my doctor. He told me to meet him at the hospital. My friend took me to the Community Hospital in Long Beach, California. Mom had gone to town for something and Jim was at work. Finally they arrived at the hospital and wanted to know why I didn't tell them how I felt. Now this was my first pregnancy, how was I to know? I felt fine when they left. Oh well, our son, Garry Dale, arrived around 3:15 a.m. January 1,1954, right on the due date. He was the first baby born in Compton, California that year. Queen for a Day was a popular TV show at that time and they sent Garry a three-piece silver set. I still have the fork and spoon.

Jim bought a semi-truck and trailer and started hauling for Livingston Rock and Gravel and Owl Rock and Gravel. We also bought our first home in Anaheim, on 2120 Victoria Avenue. That has been 46 years ago and I still remember the address. We were five miles from Disneyland and the same distance from Knottsberry Farm. Jim hauled road material to Disneyland when they were building their roads. When it opened, we could see the fireworks go off every night. Garry thought this was great. When friends came visiting, we always had the perfect places to take them. Things were going well, but still Jim wasn't around Garry as much as he should have been. Sometimes Garry would be asleep when his Dad came home from work. Jim would leave for work, sometimes as early as three and four a.m. In his spare time he was servicing his truck. But many times Jim would come by the house and take Garry on his last haul of the day.

I didn't want to raise Garry by himself, so we planned our second baby. I knew I could handle two babies. Denise was due to arrive December 13,1956. December 12, Jim went to work. I told my neighbor long before the due time that I would go to the hospital the 12th. She just didn't believe me. About eleven o'clock, December the 12th I called the same friend that took me to the hospital the first time with Garry. Then I notified my neighbor and told her I was heading for the hospital. She did see me off. Jim was a little shocked when he came in from work and learned that I was in the hospital. Mercedes' sister, Mimi, was staying with us at the time and she watched Garry during my time away. December 13th about 4 a.m. Kathryn Denise let out her first cry into this unknown world she would be living in. Both of my kids were born at the Community Hospital in Long Beach, California. They had the same nurse and the same Dr. Sinay. I believe that is the way he spelled his name. Girls, it has been forty four years ago and I can't remember all the details.

"I won't bore you girls with too much in this area. But I'll tell you a couple of things that Garry did that was rather amusing."

While I was pregnant with Denise, Garry and I would visit this large department store that wasn't too far from us. They had a large toy department. He saw a gumball machine he wanted. So I bought it and a bag of gumballs. When we got back home I gave him five pennies to play with and told him to make this last all day. I was in the kitchen cooking dinner that day and every time Garry came in he had a new gumball in his mouth. I thought, now this ain't going to work. I took all of his pennies except one. I told him when that penny was used, that was it, no more pennies. He still came in the kitchen with a new gumball in his mouth. I wonder how is he doing that. He went back to his room and I followed. I peeked around the door and saw him take his plastic, flat head screwdriver, turned the machine upside down, put the screwdriver in the slot and gave it a turn. Now Garry was under three years old. He took the penny out, put the bottom back on, turned it right side up, put that penny in and got his gum. He got his penny out again and put it on top of the gumball container for the next bout. I didn't know he would take the bottom off and keep using the same penny. When his machine was empty, he never asked for anymore gumballs.

"Girls, a person can go nuts quick enough without your kid triggering it, right? I'll tell you something else that happened when I was pregnant with Denise."

My neighbor had a girl, Linda, the same age as Garry and they were forever playing together. Garry had a red fire truck with a seat on the back that Linda would sit on. He would pedal with her up and down the sidewalk. They had a lot of fun with this little truck. One hot summer day, right after Mom and Dad left to head back to Alaska, Garry wanted to know if he could take Linda for a ride. I told him he could. Jerry and I were where we could see them, so they got in the truck and were on their way up the sidewalk. I guess Jerry and I got so involved in our conversation, that when we looked to see where the kids were, they weren't in sight. They never left the front of our houses before. Now, where are they? We ran to the nearest corner and didn't see them. Then we ran to the corner of the next block. Lo and behold, Garry and Linda were on the far side of this busy street, going in the same direction the big cars were going. Garry was giving it all he had to keep up with the big guys. A couple of cars were going real slow and we saw people laughing. Jerry and I jumped in high gear and she started stopping traffic while I got the kids off the street. Our thoughts went wild. How did he get across the street without getting hit? Why didn't someone stop and get them out of harms way? Our thoughts went on and on. That was the last time Garry raced with the big boys. I can surely see how a mother can die a thousand deaths raising their offspring.

I do believe Garry played with his guardian angels. He called them Cocoa and Dewey. We were going to Pasadena one day and when I closed the car door, Dewey didn't quite make it in. Garry started crying and said Dewey was caught in the door. I had to open the door and Garry pulled him in. The day I brought Denise home from the hospital, he stopped playing with them. As much as Garry has done, I knew they were there to protect him.

When Denise was six months old, Mom sent the kids and me a plane ticket to visit them in Anchorage. Jim took us to the Los Angeles Airport and put us on the plane. We headed for Seattle. It was getting late and Denise was already asleep. Garry was almost asleep when the stewardess came to our seats with a couple of balloons floating back and forth in mid air. That got Garry up and going full speed. We arrived at the Seattle, Washington Airport around midnight. I got my sleeping baby in my arms, my purse, my diaper bag and Garry by the hand and I didn't stop until we reached the waiting room. By now, Denise was awake. There was a stroller in the waiting room so I gently put my daughter in it. I needed a rest. Garry was like a live wire with no sleep for almost twenty-four hours. Airports weren't near as large as they are today. When they called our flight going to Anchorage, I made another grab for my baby, purse, diaper bag and Garry's hand and headed for the plane. There were no assigned seats at that time in plane history. You took whatever seat was vacant. I got us seated. Denise got back to sleep and I thought I could get a little rest. Garry and I hadn't slept in over twenty-four hours and I couldn't keep the kid in his seat. I finally had to head for the rest room. By now Denise was awake so I took her with me. They had a high chair in the rest room for babies to be belted in. I put Denise in the chair and belted her in and told Garry to watch her. When I came out of my little booth neither one was there. Now that scared me. I thought she might have been sucked out of the plane by some means. This was my first big plane trip and I was a little nervous to start with. As I left the restroom I saw Garry running toward me.

"Garry, where is Denise?" I asked hysterically.

A lady came and got her," he said, and took me to where she was.

I let out a sigh of relief. The stewardess was holding her.

We landed at the Anchorage Airport sometime that morning. When we arrived, I could see Mom and Dad waiting by the fence for us. I got my baby, purse, diaper bag and Garry by the hand and headed for the door. By now Garry was really wild. We got half way down the ramp, he turned and ran back up the ramp and grabbed a man around the leg and wouldn't let go. Mom saw I was in trouble so the gate man let her through to help me. Mom took Denise and the diaper bag and I went to free the man off Garry, which wasn't an easy job. The boy wouldn't let go of that leg. By the time I had loosened Garry's hands he would clamp his legs around the man's ankles. The man finally put his baggage down and held Garry's hands while I uncoupled the legs. When this was done, I grabbed his hand and ran down the ramp. I looked back and told the gentlemen that I was terribly sorry as I kept going toward the gate. After stopping off for breakfast, we finally arrived at my parent's home and I got the kids to bed. Garry slept twelve hours straight. Denise was pretty close on schedule.

While in Anchorage, we went back to Eagle River to experience another one of our big picnics. I saw many of my old friends, including Bob that made Anchorage their home. Bob and I did get a chance to talk a lot as he played with my kids. Bob was still single and looked to be pretty happy. It may have been just a front. That was the last time I was to see him. This trip brought back many memories. I thought, just maybe we'll come back one day and make this our home again. Things were changing slowly. New homes were being built. More people were homesteading and building homes on large tracks of wilderness land. I wanted to enjoy the thrills I once had in my share of shaping the wilds of Alaska. I yearned to hit the streams of water and pan in the old abandoned gold mines once again.

My kids would have loved it.

Time came when we should be thinking about heading back to Anaheim. I knew Jim was missing us by now. Two days before we were to leave, I woke up to see my little girl broken out in red spots. I took her to the doctor and discovered she had contracted German measles. That made our stay longer and we couldn't do anything but wait out the measles. Seems as if she got the germ from the stroller I had put her in while we were waiting for the departure of our plane in Seattle.

I had a wonderful visit in Anchorage with my Mom, Dad, Mercedes and Johnny. With the healing of my daughter, it came time to head back to Anaheim. The kids were missing their Dad, especially Garry. He missed his dad coming by the house and taking him along when he delivered his last load of gravel for the day.

Flying back home was a breeze compared to the first flight. When we arrived at the Los Angeles Airport, Garry saw his Dad walking toward us. That boy made a lunge and landed in his Dad's outstretched arms and wouldn't let go. Denise didn't care one way or the other. She was only six months old and still clung to me. We got back home and Linda was the first one to come to see Garry. I think Linda missed Garry. They ran out to the garage and piled in that fire truck for another wild ride up and down the sidewalk. Garry never left the front of the house again while peddling his fire truck.

Chapter 30

Our Move Back To Alaska

"Girls, before I met Jim, I can recall the day I walked on the black ice of a glacier. I don't know how this black part was formed. Sand, grit and dirt was all through the hard ice. It was in front of the white glacier. That wasn't scary, but getting there was."

We went passed Palmer, Alaska to this person's house and paid him to pull us across a rushing river to the Matanuska glacier. I could be wrong on the name of the glacier. He had extended a wire cable from one side of the river to the other. Then attached a pulley that was used in pulling this wide platform across the water. I can't remember having anything to hold on to as we were being pulled about four hundred feet across the water. Here I am with nothing but water rushing over huge boulders below me. Just think of my fear of heights. Seems like I can get myself in the worst situations. Believe me I held on to two peoples hands going over. Some of the people didn't go over the river. Bob was one of them that didn't make the trip. The rest of us were brave little souls. I wonder if they were afraid the lift wouldn't make it all the way. Hum-m-m.

After walking all over the black ice and taking pictures of the glacier, I was ready to go back across the river. There was no one else waiting on the bank to make the journey with me. I wanted at least one other person to show up. No luck here. I looked across to the other side and the man was sending the lift over to pick me up. I thought, oh boy, what's ole Annie going to do now? I was horrified to go it alone. But I felt like I had to get aboard since the man pulled it over for me. I eased myself upon the reeling thing and quickly laid flat on my stomach. I closed my eyes and felt my body being pulled across the water. I tried to blot out the noise the river made. When I was over the boulders, I knew this was halfway. I felt something jerk and snap and I liked to have lost control right there. I bet I made fingerprints on both sides of that board.

Thoughts can go through your mind faster than that river was flowing when you think danger is approaching. I could hear nothing but the very loud noise of the water rushing over the huge boulders. I didn't have time to shake because my arms were stretched out and my hand's were clinched tight to the edges of the board I was laying on. When I got to the other side, I was still hanging onto the edges of the board. I mean I hadn't moved. Someone touched my shoulder and I liked to have jumped off the board. I opened my eyes and Bob offered his hand to help me up.

He said, "You really are scared of heights. I thought you were kidding me."

"Bob, sometimes I don't kid around," I said as we walked back up the bank hand in hand where the others were waiting for our return home.

"Girls, this is just some fill in that happened before Jim and I were married. I have pictures of the black ice. I believe this was the Matanuska Glacier. I miss the most popular annual event of all, the week-long Anchorage Fur Rendezvous Festival held in February. They had dogsled racing, and many other contests. The week was full of fun filled merriment. I know this annual event today in the year 2001, is nothing like it was back in 1948. That is fifty three years ago," I said all in one breath. Anchorage has grown in size, and so have I.

In Anaheim, California Jim was doing very good on his new job. He had purchased this large semi-truck and trailer. His kind of work was called "outlaw trucking," because he was the owner of his truck. He hauled gravel for roads and to other projects that needed sand or gravel. After a year of hauling gravel and his semi almost paid for, rumors started circulating among the guys that their jobs my be limited. Word got out that Livingston Rock and Owl Rock was selling out to an eastern syndicate and they would use their own trucks. Jim told his friend, Curly, about this but he didn't believe him. Jim said he was selling out before the market became flooded with trucks.

Curly said, "Jim, you better hang in there, everything will get even better."

Jim sold his truck and trailer and came out good, money wise. He thought he was fortunate to retrieve all but a thousand dollars on his cab. We had already talked over this Alaskan move many times. After 5 years in the states we thought this was a good time to start making preparations to head back north and reconnect with our family ties. In June of 1957, the kids and I flew to Anchorage, and Jim drove our heavy-laden car back over the Alcan. Mom had a duplex in which she emptied one end for us to move into. What a blessing that was. Jim had no job. Mom charged us no rent because she owned the building. Jim finally found work at Merrill Field Airport.

He immediately started studying for his instructor's license. I'd have dinner ready when he came in from work. We'd eat our dinner and while he played with the kids for awhile, I'd get the kitchen in order. The kids watched TV for a short time before they were put to bed. By that time Jim would have his books on the table and studying. As many questions that I've shot at the man, you would think I could pass the test with flying colors. Well, not so. I might be able to figure out ground speed but that's all. Jim would get so flustered the books would wind up cast away in the furthest corner. This ritual went on every night. Temper, temper, temper. Most of the time everything went smooth. He went in for his test. Jim came home the next day flagging his test papers in my face and ready to take me out for dinner. "I passed! I passed! he stated with excitement.

"Do you think Granny would mind keeping the kids for two or three hours? We need to celebrate this occasion with champagne. After all I couldn't have made it without you."

Now when the man mentions an outing I don't waste any time. I knew there were three people next door that would keep the kids. At that time brother Jimmy was staying with our parents. I started getting ready. As soon as the folks came in from work I paid a visit next door. Mom was going to a college class, Jimmy offered to take them on. Dad would be going to bed early. We had a delicious dinner at the Aleutian Gardens, then we made our way over to one of the tables that circled the dance floor. We ordered champagne and just watched the dancing. One of my biggest disappointments in Jim was that he didn't dance.

I've danced all my life. In the early years in Anchorage, Mom and I would go dancing three nights a week. It was good when Dad would go with us. He never danced but he held our purses. One night a week, we went to a square dance at the base and two nights were at the Pioneer Hall, with one evening of ballroom dancing and the other was just dancing. Now Mom didn't go with me to every dance. You always had different dancing partners. John (not my brother) and I would always pair up to dance the Polka. We went to the Ambassador Club one night before the band arrived. Someone put a coin in the jukebox and came up with a lively tune. The dance floor was empty. John and I got out there and danced from one end of the floor to the other with our favorite dance, the Polka.

"Girls, it has been forty-nine years since I've danced. Bettie, the next time we go to your house we ought to have a little dance on your beautifully arranged back porch. It's certainly a large enough area," I said getting up to stretch my legs. "We should run around the house a few times to get our legs going again. I'm tired and it's not even noon. I know I have been covering some ground here, so let's take a break."

We went in the house to get our mid-morning snack and

stretch our legs a bit. Jim kept busy on his plane. He knows I don't particularly care to be interrupted when I have my mind working. We went to the living room to relax in a softer setting. I was so relaxed, I was beginning to get drowsy.

I could hear Alene say, "Let's sneak out so she can get a little rest."

"I heard that," I said, jumping up and joining them at the door. "Don't leave yet, I am only two thirds finished. Don't you want to know the ending of this?"

"Okay Annette, tell us more of Jim's adventures in bush flying." Della suggested as we trudged back to our place under this silly looking, three pronged oak tree.

Now Jim had his private and instructors license. The hard one was just ahead. He knew instrument flying but he needed a license for this one, also. Flying is a natural talent for him. But the books and tests were something else. When he came in from work, it was the same ritual night after night. I would drill him over and over. Many times the books would still land up in a disarranged mess in the same corner. We finally pulled through once again and he went in for his test. He was biting his nails waiting on the results of the test. Finally he was called in. Of course he was nervous. When he got the news he had passed, he came home with another celebration on his mind. Now he could legally do it all. It seemed like most of the small planes in Alaska did all types of bush work. A bush pilot flies out where there are no roads. You are really in the boonys. He has flown on skis, wheels and floats, year round in all kinds of weather. He went from Merrill Field to Lake Hood. Lake Hood is a big lake just outside of Anchorage. From there he flew for the Pure Oil Company. His last job with Pure Oil was the end of the Aleutian Islands, Cold Bay Alaska.

"Before I get too far along here, I'll tell you some shenanigans he has pulled."

While he was still with Piper Company at Merrill Field, he

went to test a plane out that the mechanics had just worked on. He asked the gas boy if he wanted to go with him. The young man jumped at the chance to fly. Jim was sailing through the air with the greatest of ease, when he saw some ducks meeting him in flight. Jim thought the ducks would move over but they didn't. One came through the windshield. Jim leaned his head to one side and the duck hit his shoulder and landed in the boy's lap in the back seat. Now that was one scared young man. He sat there and didn't say a word. Jim had all of his attention on this pretty large hole in the windshield and keeping the plane in the air. He turned the plane around and headed back to the airport. The young man was still in shock and couldn't talk. He alighted from the plane and went to the office white as a sheet. Jim walked in behind him and stated what happen. Needless to say the gas boy never flew with Jim again. I never did get the blood out of Jim's jacket.

A pilot told this on Jim, but somehow I never believed it. As I have said, Jim's job took him all over Alaska. One guy approached him one day to take him way back in the boonys to his cabin. Of course, he had a goodly supply of items plus a cat. Jim told the man he'd better put the cat in a container of some sort. The guy said he'd hold the cat in his lap and she would be all right. They got about halfway into this wilderness country and the vibration of the plane got the cat off of the man's lap. The cat started circling the cab. Now this was getting on Jim's nerves and he told the man to catch the cat and keep her calm. The man tried to catch the feline but couldn't. By now Jim was mad. The next round the cat made, Jim opened the window and the cat sailed out into the air. The fellow didn't say a word. When they arrived at his cabin Jim said, "Don't worry about the cat, they always land on their feet and she'll find her way home."

Jim was flying back from somewhere and as he flew over this mountain, he saw something white lying on the ground. He circled and came in to get a closer look. It was a dead goat. Jim thought, hey this will make me a little extra money. He knew the Fish and Wildlife would hire him to take Jack to get the goat. He landed at Merrill Field and went in the office to call the Fish and Wildlife commission and talked to his friend, Jack. Jim told him about the dead goat on the mountainside.

Jack inquired, "Jim, can you land on a mountainside that steep?"

Jim said, "No problem." He used that expression a lot.

Jack met Jim at the airport and from there they started their journey to check out the dead goat on a mountain that probably no human had been before. Jim thought it was exciting to be the first person somewhere. At that time in history he may have been right. Jim has never been lost in the wild. As they approached the mountain they saw their target.

Jack got somewhat nervous as they were heading closer to the side of the mountain. He thought he was getting mighty close to meeting his Maker.

Jim said, "Jack, when we land, you jump out and hang on to the tail and don't let the plane roll down the mountain."

Jim cut the engine and landed the plane like a fly would light on a wall. Jack jumped out and as Jim made his dive out he grabbed his shovel and started digging holes for the front wheels to fit in. When the plane was secured they went and checked the dead goat. Jack cut the head off and put it in a plastic bag to be checked by their lab technicians. When you are out in the wilderness you have to goof off a little bit. They talked about how they would depart from this mountain slope. One thing Jack knew was that he would have to walk down to the valley below.

They got the plane turned around facing downward. Jack had to hold the tail while Jim ran, jumped in and got the engine going. As the plane sailed off down the mountainside, Jack started making his way to the valley below. They made a lot of pictures that day. I think wherever Jack is, he would still be showing the pictures of that eventful day back in the late fifties. I know Jim projects his copies on the screen whenever he finds an interested person.

"Annette, we'd like to see those pictures sometime. Do you think Jim can find time to show them to us?" asked Bettie. You know my husband was a pilot during the second war. Flying has always intrigued me."

"Bettie, it would be the highlight of his day. Pick the time when you gals want to sit and enjoy our color slides of Alaska," I said smiling at the thought of me being a part of this rough frontier land.

Jim and another pilot were flying around somewhere and heard this SOS call. They were nearby, so Jim answered the call. They located the plane that was in trouble and followed it until the pilot ditched his plane on the beach. Jim landed close by on the same beach. He and his friend went to check the ditched plane, and saw the pilot was shaken up but not hurt. After checking his plane to see what damage was done, Jim flew him back to Anchorage. I think this happened in the Bristol Bay area. The pilot went back the next day to check and see what went wrong. When he got there he found his engine missing and some of the instruments. I don't know if the thieves were ever caught.

When Jim was flying for Pure Oil Company, the boss gave the men a day off from their seismograph jobs. He told Jim to take the guys across the water to this beer joint. The boss thought these rugged men needed a break. Jim went to prepare the plane for the flight to the nearest island that had a bar. The plane could only carry about five men at a time so Jim made several trips.

It came time to start the process of bringing boozed up men back to home base. He did all right until the second load. There was one man pretty drunk and he wanted to head back on this flight. Jim wouldn't let him in the plane until he sobered up some. He left him for later baggage.

When he went back for his last load, this guy was drunker

than ever. Jim knew he wasn't going to make the trip back for one drunk. As the remainder of men started getting in the plane, this drunk started to climb in. Jim grabbed him by the shirt collar, took him to the edge of the water and started dunking his head in the water.

"Now remember girls, this is Alaska and the water is always cold."

Jim would dunk his head in the water and bring him back up, take a look at him and dunk him in again until he looked like he wouldn't puke in the plane. Jim finally got him in and seated. Not one word was exchanged all the way back to home base.

Jim has done some risky things. He seemed to fly planes out of difficult situations that no one else wanted to do. One guy had his plane on a little lake and wanted to get it out. He asked Jim if he would come get it and take it to Merrill Field. The guy took Jim to his house. They went to the lake, which was surrounded by trees, and Jim checked everything out and said, "Yes, I can get it out. They gassed the plane up and Jim got in. He coasted to the widest side, revved the engine up high enough to clear the trees. The man met him back at Merrill Field. To me, Jim took a lot of chances, but to him it was "no problem."

Another man had his plane back in the boon-docks on floats. It had snowed and it was pretty deep. This man wanted his plane out so he could get skis put on it. He asked Jim if he could get it out with the floats on. Jim said, "No problem." They pulled the plane to the road. Jim got in and took off down the road and was airborne in no time flat. He landed at Merrill Field on a strip of snow that was for planes with skis, because they kept the landing strips free of snow.

Chapter 31

Four Guys Looking For Gold

"You know ladies, Jim knew what he flew inside out. He was a very good pilot. He could take off and land on a dime and leave a nickel sticking out. I'll tell you about one of his dumb pranks, if it can be called a prank."

When Jim became bored around camp, he would get in the Cessna and go find a big brownie. Now this is a very large brown bear. When one was located he would start buzzing this animal. Jim would see how close he could come without getting too low. The brownie would stand up, slapping at the plane. Mister bear would get so mad he would tear up the hillside. Jim just kept on teasing this large animal. His last dive put Jim a little to close for comfort. He came a few inches of getting knocked out of the air as mister bear made a swipe at the left wing. He came up sweating a tad on this one. He left the brownie in complete frustration. Jim flew in the opposite direction of the camp before returning to home base. He always had these little bouts with the bears a long way from camp. If the bear had knocked him out of the air, Jim would have been in grave danger. The bear would have been so mad by this time he would have swallowed Jim whole and burped him back up in little pieces.

Jim always got our moose meat for winter. When you cut a steak off the hip it seemed to take two plates to hold the thing. I could make Swiss steak from moose meat that tasted like beef. How good it tasted and how tender it was.

"Ladies, I bought eight ivory handled steak knives in 1949. I watched an Eskimo artist sketch the first design on the ivory of one knife handle. Each etching is different. That guy was great. I never put these knives to use anymore. They are certainly a fond memory of my early days in Alaska."

Jim and his three buddies knew there was gold in "them thar hills". A man that found signs of gold needed heavy equipment to get it out of the ground. There was no way to get what he needed that high on this mountain. These four flying buddies were positive they could locate the area it was in. With four strong backs to handle the job, they just knew they would be rich in no time flat. They had a plan. They rolled up their mining tools and all they would need, like food, cooking utensils, and extra clothes in their sleeping bags. Jim met the guys at Merrill Field Airport. They loaded their gear in the plane. One of his buddies went with him. As Jim flew over their campsite, Pete threw the bags out the door. They flew back to the airport where the other two men were waiting. Then the four men got in the car and drove as far as they could up the mountain they were to ascend. They finally arrived at their designated site. All their gear was found except Jim's. They looked all over the mountainside and never found Jim's bed roll. There is no telling where his sleeping bag scooted to, probably in some deep fissure. I have often wondered what had happened to my gold pan and pick, now I know. They never found the mother lode either. They found gold dust and some nuggets but nothing to prompt them to make the journey back up the mountain. That night the guys gave Jim their blankets to sleep under. I know it was pretty cold that high up. That weekend they trudged back down the mountain with their packs on their backs. They got into the car they had abandoned three days earlier and went to their homes completely exhausted.

"I'll tell you ladies something that really happened long before we appeared on the Alaskan scene."

One day an old prospector came into town to get his supply of groceries. All prospectors seem to have a little burro for their pack animal. As they were coming back across the glacier the burro fell into a crevasse. He knew he'd never see his food and the burro again. He made his way back to town for more supplies. That was a long journey for an old man. Not too many months after that incident, he was making his way out to stock his food shelf once more. He happened to look in the valley below and saw his burro grazing on the new grass. When he made his way to the valley he was surprised to see most of his items were still strapped on the burro's back. He just turned around and went back to his cabin with his burro in tow. He knew he could make the trip later that year. You know, it's a wonder that burro didn't freeze.

There are times when I would walk around pulling my hair wondering where my kids were. The thing was I was always with them. My little girl disappeared right before my eyes. She never went outside the fence. But she was missing. Soooo, Garry and I looked all around the yard. We searched each room, I looked high and he looked low. No Denise. I was beginning to feel a frantic mood coming over me. I got where I couldn't talk. Garry stood back and watched me speed up going from room to room once again. I happened to stop by the bed and noticed a little hump in the covers. All I could see was a little nose sticking out. I stopped long enough to thank God she was safe at home. By the time I calmed down, Garry was beside me. I pointed to her nose sticking out from under the quilt and Garry got tickled. I headed him out before we both woke her up.

Chapter 32

Alaska Becomes a State

June 30,1958 congress voted to admit Alaska to the Union. Alaskans held celebrations throughout the territory. January 3, 1959 President Dwight D. Eisenhower issued a proclamation making Alaska the 49th state. That was some celebration. They had the largest bonfire I have ever witnessed. If I'm not mistaken they had a log from each of the lower 48. They had a huge flag on the side of one of the buildings with 49 stars. It seemed like when Anchorage gave a festival, it would last a few days. Dad brought home a green bottle of liquor shaped like a star. Of course he drank the liquor and gave Mom the bottle, which I still have.

Garry entered the Mountain View Grade School in 1961. He was so proud. Denise and I took him to and from school each day. I noticed a little girl holding Garry's hand each evening when he came to the car. Every day it was a different girl hanging on him. One day Garry got in the car and said, "Mom, I don't know why, but girls fight over who is going to hold my hand every day."

I asked, "Garry, do you encourage them?"

He came back with, "No, but I like Ruth the best."

"Okay, you girls know I have done some dumb things in my life, but I can tell you one that puts extra icing on the cake. And the worse thing was Jim didn't stop me."

Jim was flying for Pure Oil Company way out on the far end of the Aleutian Islands, namely Cold Bay. I got the idea of moving to Oregon. It would be just as close to Jim as Anchorage was, and a whole lot cheaper, since Mom was selling the duplex.

Before Jim and I were married, Jim promised me that we would sit down and discuss major issues. My folks and I always talked over our next move. Jim was in the Air Force for so many years he got used to them telling him what to do.

Dad would drive out with the kids and me. Our belongings would be sent out by ship and rail. Dad had already retired from the Alaska Railroad and Mom would be retiring the next year. We relocated in Grants Pass, Oregon. I went to a used furniture store and bought enough to furnish our two-bedroom house we would call home for a few months. I got Garry back in school and Denise in kindergarten.

"Bettie, you know I like to make wine. I'll tell you one of my earliest experiences." While we were in Grants Pass, I asked Dad if he would show me how to make wine. He kinda liked the idea, so I set out to find some grapes. I brought in about a bushel and we went to work on getting them prepared. We extracted a few quarts of deep purple juice. Then we added sugar to taste and set it aside to start fermenting. It set there in two one-gallon glass jugs for a week with no noticeable action.

During this time Mom called from Anchorage and wanted us to look for some land that would be adequately suited for their retirement. We looked over many parcels of land. We left our address at one of the Realtors to see what they could find for us. During this waiting period our wine just sat there in limbo.

Dad said, "I know what we can do." And he headed for the wine jugs.

We took the stuff to the bathroom, turned the gas heater on and closed the door. Dad said that would get it going. It just needed to be warmer. But that didn't get the fermentation started either. So we took our jugs of juice to the kitchen and filled the sink as high as we could with warm water hoping that would get the action started. Garry was in school and Denise was playing in the backyard. Dad and I were relaxing in the living room with magazines opened to some interesting stories. We saw a car drive up and Dad pushed in high gear. I've never seen a sixty-three year old man move so fast.

He said hysterically, "Someone has smelled our wine and they have sent the revenue officers after us. Let's hide this stuff fast."

I thought the man was going to pour it down the sink. Dad was almost sweating. He had seen the revenue officers in action back in the hills of Arkansas with the illegal bootleggers. My Dad could see himself spending his retirement in some jail cell over a little wine. We got it hid just as the door bell rang. I went to the door while Dad re-opened his magazine and pretended to read.

The lady said she was from this certain real estate office and she had a tract of land she wanted to show us. She came in for awhile and Dad set back completely at ease. I got Denise and Dad in our car and I followed this lady to a beautiful five- acre tract. I got the needed information and sent it to Mom. She never bought land in Oregon. We got back to the house and Dad and I just had to laugh a bit about the rush on our wine. We finally got it to ferment without the yeast. I can not bring to memory what the stuff tasted like. I know one thing, we didn't let it go to waste.

I had bought furniture but our household things hadn't arrived yet. It took a long time by boat and truck to get our necessities to us in Grants Pass. Before I got the boxes unpacked Jim called and said for us to get back to Anchorage. I got the same trucking company that brought our boxes to us to haul them back to Seattle. From there they were sent back over the water and then by rail to Anchorage. Jim had a nice mobile home waiting for us and we were back in business with our family together once again. Poor Garry, no wonder he hated school so bad.

"Ladies, I'll tell you a few quickies that are not long and strung out."

I had a bronzing business that I operated from a small building in the backyard when we lived in Mt. View, Alaska. Mt. View was about two or three miles out of Anchorage. I bronzed all kinds of things. I made peanut earrings, pretzel pins, english walnut half pins. I bronzed baby shoes and mounted some of them on picture frames connected to an ashtray. A young man on crutches sold the earrings and pins for me. He got half of what he sold. We were both happy.

The kids and I were heading for a movie one cold day. Just before we got to the signal light the thing turned yellow. There was a complete sheet of ice at this crossing so I started braking. When I did, the car turned completely around in perfect alignment in the left lane. It just so happened that I was the only one at the crossing at that time. I just gradually put the pedal to the metal and we went back home. The kids thought that I was some cool dude to be able to do something like that. They couldn't wait to tell their daddy. I sat over in the corner chair to see what kind of reaction that would come from him.

He just said, "Yeah, really! Was it really a perfect turn?"

Today the kids have forgotten the bravery of this little stunt lady.

I kept two little boys once while their mother worked. They were smart kids but hard headed little dudes. Those boys and Denise played well together. I had a big picture window on both sides of the living room and they were always in sight. One day I looked out and the boys were fighting. I saw Denise go over to them and they put their heads together in a conversation of some sort. The next thing I saw was Bobby taking her right hand and Tony the left one. They came on in without another cross word. When they entered the house I asked Denise what were they fussing about.

She said, "They were fighting over me. Tony didn't want Bobby holding my hand."

I asked her what did she say that changed their mind.

She said, "I told Tony to hold one hand and Bobby the other one. That made them happy."

I asked her, "How did you feel about it?"

"Mom, I started to come on in and just let the dumb boys fight. They like to fight anyway."

I am sure you ladies have played with those little jumping beans, right? I bought Garry some one day. When he got tired of seeing and feeling them jump, he put the things on the counter. Denise brought them to me that day and wanted to know what was in there to make them jump.

"I don't really know, honey. They may be little monsters trying to get out," I said teasingly.

I shouldn't have said that. The next day Garry started looking for his beans and wanted to know if I had seen them. I told him no, I hadn't seen them. Denise walked up and I asked her if she knew where the beans were.

"Mom, you said there were monsters in them trying to get out, so I flushed them down the toilet," Denise said eyeing Garry sharply just in case he made a mad dash for her to wring her neck.

He never mentioned them again and never asked for any more jumping beans.

It's amazing how you think back on cherished memories of your children. It was a cold wintry day about 30 degrees below outside. Denise decided to stay in that day and help me make French bread. Just as I was taking the bread out of the oven, Garry walked in the front door. He looked at me with those big blue eyes and said even before he put his schoolbooks down, "Mom, I bet you are the only mom in town that has hot French bread waiting for their boy when he comes in from school."

He put his books down and came over and gave me one of the biggest hugs. I put the butter on the table. Denise already had two plates out. Garry started slicing bread. Those kids ate almost a whole loaf of bread that was still hot enough to melt the butter.

"Coming in from the cold to a warm house, smelling yeast bread right out of the oven, I tell you girls, that gets your taste buds working."

"You ladies are probably tired of me talking so much about my past, but come to think of it you have been trying to get me started for a long time, right?" I said.

Chapter **33**

The 1964 Earthquake

"You haven't told us anything about the earthquake yet," said Bettie. "I know there is more than what you are telling us."

"The earthquake happened a year after we left Alaska. I'll tell you all I know about it if Alene will pour me a glass of wine. This is blackberry wine I made six months ago. Do you like it?" I asked holding my glass up to see the pretty berry color. "This is one of my best batches."

We came out for good on February 1963 in a Volkswagen. Believe me we had some tense moments on that trip. But that's another story.

The quake hit Anchorage 1964, and I believe on Good Friday. Mom and Dad, Jimmy and my family were all stateside. Mom was going crazy by not hearing from Johnny and his family. Back in Anchorage Johnny had, I think, a friend that had a ham radio set. A person in Seattle heard the message and called Mom and told her that Johnny and his family were okay.

After many days, we started hearing from our people. Remember BB, my aunt that we took up with us in 1948? She was still there. Aunt Blanche had broken her ankle and she hadn't been downtown in a month or more. A friend of hers thought she would take her downtown for an outing and check out their new store, I believe it was Pennys that hadn't been open too long. There Aunt Blanche was, hopping around on her trusty crutches. After a tiring hour of walking around they thought they would cross the street and go in Pennys. Before they got halfway across the street the light turned yellow. Aunt Blanche told her friend she was going to turn around and go back, because she couldn't make it across before the light turned red. They went back and stood by a parking meter and the next minute everything in front of them sank. They saw the wall fall from the new Penny's store. Auntie's friend hugged her around that parking meter so hard it broke one of her ribs. Now she had a broken rib and ankle. I know that smarted, but if they had kept going across the street they would have been killed.

Back at Johnny's house, he was laying on the couch and it started moving around. Dishes shot out of the cabinets and broke. The cat started making circles around the living room. Johnny finally staggered to the door to let the cat out and before he could open the storm door the cat shot out the hole where there was no pane of glass. That cat didn't come back home for days. Don't you know that was some scared cat. Looks like it took that long for her to get over her scare.

"I will tell you ladies one thing I'm thankful for. I missed a hurricane in Pascagoula in 1947 and a dust storm in one of the northern states. The dust was still thick enough to stifle you. We missed the Yellowstone National Park earthquake by one day. My family and I went through this forest fire in Canada in 49, and of course, we missed the earthquake in Anchorage by a year. That was close enough for me. With the near misses I've had, I'm thankful God has granted me with the years I've had. Me being so shy most of my life I feel cheated. But could I have been the person I am if I was any different? There is no telling where my path would have taken me."

I went to Alaska as a true Cheechako, one who is as green as grass, and came out a confirmed Sourdough. When I arrived in Anchorage I met a few of the "intelligent" males. A couple of them wanted to know if I knew what I had to do to be a sourdough. I was all ears and anxious to know, because I wanted to be one. I wanted to join this big circle of sourdoughs. They said I had to kill a bear, sleep with an Eskimo, and pee in the Yukon.

My eyes slowly went from one to the other and I said, "Reeeeally?" I thought they would laugh themselves silly. They thought they had me going. I asked them if they had become sourdoughs yet. I think all they did was sleep with an Eskimo. I told them I was going to hang in there and come out a firm Sourdough.

"Now you girls know me a little better. I have had plenty of ups and downs in my life. Some miserable times but most were happy ones. I can look back on a lot that I have done and wished that I could change things, but that's life.

I can look back on my life and see where God has protected me on my long journey. When I would fall, He would pick me up, brush me off, nudge me down the right path and say, go girl, you can make it.

I have told you girls all the good, and some not so good about me. I have taken you from the dark depression days to the bright side of prosperity. I have incorporated most of my life's adventures, and ladies that's about it.

"So, I thank you, my dearest friends for hearing me out, brave little souls that you are. Let's go out for lunch. It's on me. I'll tell Jim we'll be gone for awhile."

If your bookstore does not stock this book,
order from
Annette Edwards
A SAGA OF A CHEECHAKO CLAN
P.O. Box 415 Bryant, Arkansas 72089

Each book is $15.00 including postage and handling. Send check or money order to the above address. No cash or c.o.d.'s please.

Amount enclosed _____

Name ________________________________
Address ______________________________
City ____________ State __________ Zip ________

Please allow four to six weeks for delivery.